HOPE
For Hurting Relationships

HOPE
For Hurting Relationships

Myron Rush

This book is designed for your personal reading pleasure and profit. It is also intended for group study. A Leader's Guide with Reproducible Response Sheets is available from your local bookstore or from the publisher.

VICTOR BOOKS®

A DIVISION OF SCRIPTURE PRESS PUBLICATIONS INC.
USA CANADA ENGLAND

Unless otherwise indicated, all Scripture quotations are from the *Holy Bible, New International Version,* © 1973, 1978, 1984, International Bible Society. Used by permission of Zondervan Bible Publishers. Others are from *The Living Bible* (TLB), © 1971, Tyndale House Publishers, Wheaton, IL 60189.

Recommended Dewey Decimal Classification: 248.4
Suggested Subject Heading: CONDUCT OF CHRISTIAN LIFE

Library of Congress Catalog Card Number: 88-062854
ISBN: 0-89693-643-0

VICTOR BOOKS
A division of SP Publications, Inc.
Wheaton, IL 60187

CONTENTS

AUTHOR'S NOTE

Some of the names of people and places mentioned in this book have been changed to protect both the innocent and the guilty. I trust as you read this book you will focus on how you can apply the principles presented to your role in relationships, instead of thinking how they apply to someone else's. There is hope for both hurting relationships and hurting people whose relationships have been destroyed. For such people, this book was written for you and to you.

Myron D. Rush

RELATIONSHIP PROBLEMS: A GROWING EPIDEMIC

1

When I first met Janice Stone she was a very bitter woman. And like all people consumed with bitterness, she felt she had a right to be.

Janice's whole life had evolved around the church. Her parents spent almost 40 years on the South American mission field where Janice was born and lived until she came to the United States to attend Bible college.

Janice had doubts about coming to the United States to attend college. As the baby of the family she had always been close to her parents, and the thought of being away from them disturbed her greatly. However, her parents and other missionary friends assured her it was the right thing to do if she felt God wanted her to be a pastor's wife.

Her senior year in college she married Charles Stone, the most popular and promising future pastor on campus. He was class president his first three years of college and student body president his fourth. Janice had been editor of the college paper and student government association member her junior and senior years. They were married the day after graduation and after a short honeymoon moved to a Midwestern farming community to pastor a small rural church.

Charles and Janice were as popular with people in the community as they had been in college and within a couple of years the church had more than doubled in size and started a building project. Shortly after the new building was completed, Charles was offered the job of pastoring a rapidly growing church in Florida.

Janice hated the thought of moving away from friends, but she was committed to Charles and their goal of developing an effective church ministry in a metropolitan community. Therefore, she was just as excited as Charles in looking forward to their new home and the challenges of a growing and progressive church.

According to Janice, the next ten years were the happiest time of her life. They had two children, a girl and boy, and Charles' ministry was so successful they soon had one of the largest churches in the city.

Janice and Charles made a good team. They were attractive and outgoing people and each had an effective ministry—Charles in the church and Janice as a talk-show host on a local Christian radio station. Janice often spoke to womens groups on a subject popular within church circles, "How to be a supportive wife."

Charles and Janice Stone represented the model of success among their Christian friends and sometimes envious onlookers. However, at the very pinnacle of their highly productive careers Janice's world came crashing down and her life changed forever.

For weeks Charles had been counseling one of the wealthiest and most influential couples in the church. Late one evening Charles and the man's wife were caught in a compromising position on a remote beach. The next day the story was local front page news, and before the week's end Charles and his newfound lady friend had left town together, supposedly headed for California.

Janice not only found herself alone, but to her surprise, the focus of much criticism. Many of her supposed friends were both openly and secretly accusing her of driving her husband to another woman. Some said she should have been at home instead of out running seminars on how to be a supportive wife. Others argued that she spent too much time working on her talk show and not enough time dealing with the demands of her marriage.

Unable to cope with the shattering events in her life, Janice sent her children to her sister's for the summer, packed a few belongings into the back of her car, and moved to Denver, Colorado to live with her recently divorced cousin.

"And that's my story!" Janice sighed, picking up an old copy of *National Geographic* as we waited in the counseling clinic office. The blizzard-like conditions of the snowy January morning in Denver had caused both of our counselors to be late for our weekly appointments.

Though it had been two years since her husband's unfaithfulness caused her world to crumble, Janice was still an emotional "basket case." She was an angry and bitter person, disgusted with people—especially Christians—and life in general. Her son had gone to live with his grandparents after their retirement from the mission field. And from the sound of her story, Janice was having a hard time handling her daughter.

During that cold, dreary morning Janice Stone stared out the window as if talking to the blowing snow. As she nervously pulled at a string on the cuff of her blouse, tears mingled with blue mascara streamed down her cheeks. At times I wondered if she was aware of my presence, less than four feet from her, as she again, for the umpteenth time, relived the painful events of the past. Janice was obviously experiencing a great deal of hurt, frustration, and emotional pain.

I not only sympathized with Janice; I empathized as well. Watching her tears flow and listening to the despair in her voice brought back the painful memory of my own marriage failure. I had felt the same feelings. I experienced the misunderstanding and rejection of close friends in the Christian community. I watched an effective ministry that I had poured my life into be almost destroyed. My own daughter and son rebelled from the hurt and lashed out at me and their mother, frustrated by the emotional pain of the divorce. I knew the tortuous feeling of failure that accompanies the breakup of a relationship. Like Janice Stone, I also wanted to give up on people and life in general. Yet through all the dark days of despair and emotionally damaging experiences, I discovered that there truly is hope.

The Purpose of This Book

My work is dedicated to the growing multitude of people living with mental hurts and scars that have left them emotionally crippled in their relationships with others. This book offers hope to those who believe their relationships with others are hopeless—or about to become so.

On the following pages I will explore such issues as: why we form the relationships we do; the evolving relationship cycle; the types of relationship styles; why relationships deteriorate; how they can be restored; the steps to open communication; how to handle relationship failure; and finally, how to turn your relationship failures into positive experiences that will enable you to develop and maintain rewarding relationships now and in the future.

We All Have Problems

From time to time we all experience problems in our relationships. One of the first, but most important points we must learn when dealing with others is that there are no perfect relationships. "They lived happily ever after" exists only on the pages of fairy tales.

However, that does not mean we cannot have good—and even great—relationships with others. But it is unrealistic to assume that we can ever develop problem-free relationships. Realizing that we will always face problems in our relationships, my purpose is to help you understand why those problems developed, how to minimize their effect on the relationship, and how to learn from them to build stronger, more productive relationships in the future.

I was extremely reluctant in writing this book because of my own problems in relationships. My life is no example to follow. I failed in a marriage relationship. Because of my inability to get along with fellow employees, I once lost a job. I have not always related properly to my children. And unfortunately, I have not always maintained a right relationship with God. However, from those mistakes and failures I have learned a great deal about what makes relationships go right and wrong.

I write as someone who has walked ahead along the painful road of destroyed or deteriorating relationships. I have walked that lonely, dark path and I can tell you that there definitely is *hope for hurting relationships*. I know because I have lived it.

Like Janice Stone, I too have experienced the bitterness that sometimes develops in the aftermath of a relationship failure. I have experienced the feeling of utter worthlessness that engulfs those who try and try again, but fail to make their most important relationships work.

I share my mistakes with you to highlight two important points at the beginning of this book. First, we all make mistakes and experience failure in our relationships, and second, no matter how great the problem or severe the pain, there is always hope for tomorrow.

Relationship Problems Are on the Increase

A popular philosophy prevalent today tells us that the world is on the threshold of a great New Age in which humankind will live in peace, harmony, and love. However, American trends during this century would indicate the opposite is true. Relationship problems have reached epidemic proportions during the last few years, and statistics reveal that they are getting worse, not better.

According to the United States Department of Commerce's 1987 edition of the *Statistical Abstract of the United States* (published by the U.S. Government Printing Office in Washington, D.C.), in 1910 there was approximately one divorce for every 10 marriages in this country. By 1985 there was approximately one divorce for every two marriages. That means that during the past 75 years the divorce rate in this country has skyrocketed from 10 percent to almost 50 percent. In addition, the number of people living together out of wedlock has increased almost 400 percent, just since 1970.

The same government document points out that for the 10-year period between 1976–1985 violent crime increased by 32.2 percent, forcible rape increased 53 percent, and aggravated assault increased 44.5 percent. During the same time period, reported child abuse cases increased by almost 80 percent.

These are frightening statistics that indicate relationship problems in this country have reached epidemic proportions. It is ironic during this century of great technological advancement that we have apparently forgotten most of what we knew about developing and maintaining human relationships. We paraded into the 20th century on the backs of horses and are preparing to leave it on the vapor trails of rocket ships. However, as the century draws to a close, it seems we have regressed instead of progressed in our ability to relate to one another.

The Source of Relationship Problems

Every person experiencing serious relationship problems inevitably asks the haunting question, "Why me?" During my first conversation with Janice Stone that snowy, cold, January day she asked, "Why did this happen to me? Can you please tell me why?" However, I sensed she really didn't expect an answer.

Relationship problems are as old as humankind. From the time of Cain's slaying of Abel human history has been littered with relational problems. Our history books are filled with the results of such disastrous relationships. Wars have been fought, nations destroyed, and countless innocent people killed because of our inability to get along with one another.

The cause lies in one horrible manifestation of our fallen human nature—selfishness. *Problems in relationships result when individuals are so committed to their own views and values that they ignore and neglect those of others.* No matter what kind of psychological or philosophical jargon we use to camouflage this hideous destroyer of humanity; in the final analysis it is still the deadly sin of selfishness. Self-centeredness is the greatest enemy the human race has ever faced. Selfishness is a greater threat to the existence of humanity on this planet than all the doomsday predictions.

A once-popular cigarette commercial—"I'd rather fight than switch"—accurately captures man's commitment to his own

14

views and values. All of us have that tendency. We'd rather hurt another than stop feeding our own selfish interests. For short periods of time, especially if we need to prove a point, we may put the interests of others ahead of our own. But our natural tendency is to put our needs and interests ahead of those of others. It's what we call "human nature"; the Bible describes this as our "carnal nature" or "the natural man."

Social scientists would tell us selfishness is the result of our "self-preservation instincts" at work. They would attempt to quiet our guilt regarding such behavior by telling us that such self-protection is only a normal and natural action. However, the Bible clearly points out that all selfishness and self-centeredness is sin. Philippians 2:3-4 addresses the problem of selfishness head-on stating, "Do nothing out of selfish ambition or vain conceit, but in humility consider others better than yourselves. Each of you should look not only to your own interests, but also to the interests of others."

This passage is the foundation on which all our relationships should be built. If we could apply the principles of these verses consistently, our relationships would be productive and rewarding experiences. Therefore, I will continually refer us back to this very important passage because it holds the key to healthy relationships. The pain, hurt, and misery we sometimes experience is a direct result of violating the principles presented in Philippians 2:3-4.

For example, shortly after I was married I decided to impress my new bride by doing the breakfast dishes. I was convinced my young wife would realize how fortunate she was to have such a great guy as me for a husband. However, as I busied myself with the task my wife came into the kitchen and began suggesting how I could improve my dishwashing. I immediately became defensive, and as she continued to explain my defensiveness turned to anger.

Upon coming into the kitchen she said, "Myron, you're getting water all over the floor!" I immediately thought, "It's no big deal. I'll clean it up when I'm through." However, before I could respond she started to carefully stack the dishes in the drainer so they would not fall onto the counter.

I said, "Look! You do it your way and I'll do it mine, OK?" Taking the dish towel out of my hand she said, "Oh, Myron! Don't be so stubborn!" I threw the dishcloth into the water and informed my new wife that I had washed lots of dishes before she came along and certainly didn't need her advice on stacking dishes in the drainer.

The discussion that followed developed into a major argument concerning the best way to stack dishes. Our own unbending self-centeredness caused us to allow this situation of little—if any—importance to ruin our whole day.

In the final analysis the real issue wasn't the best way to stack dishes, but whether or not we were willing to put the other person first in accord with Philippians 2:3-4. We became so committed to our own ideas, methods, and opinions that we were unwilling to listen to those of the other person—even when it involved such a minor point as how to stack dishes in the drainer. Isn't it amazing how destructive selfishness can be when our own "self" is threatened? Selfish attitudes have the power to inflict a mortal blow to any relationship given enough time and the right opportunity.

My wife and I had been so committed to our own views, values, and versions that when those were challenged we became defensive and protective of our own "self." When we adopt such a posture we become all the more unwilling to accept someone else's needs.

Webster's dictionary defines selfishness as "the exclusive consideration by a person of his own interests." The Philippians passage warns against overemphasis on self. Throughout the pages of this book I will continually emphasize this point: *Failure to consider the interests of others is the major cause of problems in all interpersonal relationships.*

The Five Laws of Interpersonal Relationships
As an observer of human nature I believe that there are certain laws that tend to govern all interpersonal relationships. These laws are stated as follows:

▶ All relationships revolve around personal needs.
▶ Contact alters relationships.
▶ Relationships are continually changing.
▶ Fulfilled needs build relationships.
▶ Unfulfilled needs erode relationships.

Let's consider each of these laws and observe how they influence and affect relationships.

All relationships revolve around personal needs. We all need other people. In fact, some of our needs can only be met through relationships with others. For example, when God created Adam He placed him in a perfect environment, the Garden of Eden. Adam had a perfect relationship with his Creator. He was living in a disease-free environment. He could live forever. Adam never lacked for food. He lived in harmony with his beautiful world. A perfect man was living in a perfect world and maintaining a perfect relationship with his God—what more could one need?

Yet Adam did have unmet needs. He was alone. Adam had no one to share his beautiful paradise. He had no spiritual or physical needs; however, he was not emotionally complete. He needed another.

Recently I drove from Anchorage, Alaska to my home in Colorado. It was a beautiful trip. For 4,000 miles I traveled through some of the most beautiful scenery in the world. I saw huge glaciers carving their way down the sides of towering, snow-covered mountains. I saw moose, caribou, and bear by the beautiful lakes and rivers in the endless, majestic, mountain valleys. It was beauty beyond description; however, I was traveling alone with no one to share this great experience.

And yet that experience cannot begin to compare with Adam's situation. I at least met people at campgrounds, rest stops, and gas stations along the way. I could listen to people on the radio and wave to them as they passed on the road. However, Adam was totally alone without the benefit of human contact.

God realized man's need for personal relationships. Therefore, in Genesis 2:18 He said, "It is not good for the man to be

17

alone. I will make a helper suitable for him." Notice Adam's response when he awoke from his deep sleep and found Eve there. "This is now bone of my bone and flesh of my flesh" (Gen. 2:23). Can't you just imagine the enthusiasm in those words. Adam was overjoyed. He now had another person like himself. One of his greatest needs had been met.

Try to imagine Adam's frustration in trying to converse with the various animals and share his feelings as he lived each day. At last Adam could express his thoughts to someone like himself, who was capable of understanding what was inside of him. Adam's beautiful environment was of little value to him unless there was someone with which to share it.

Notice God said, "It is not good for the man to be alone" (Gen. 2:18). God recognized Adam had needs that could only be met through relationships with another person. You and I have needs that can only be met through relationships with others. That is the way God made us. Our emotional makeup is such that we all need other people. No one is a complete person apart from other people. The reason we form relationships is to meet the needs of one another.

Contact alters relationships. Relationships develop through contact with others. Day-to-day contact continually alters our relationships. Your contact with fellow employees each day changes those relationships. The daily contact you have with your children or mate alters those relationships. The contact you have with God daily changes that relationship. The quality of your relationship with another is determined by the type of interaction that occurs between you and the other person.

Relationships are continually changing. Since our contact continually alters our relationships that means they are continually changing. Relationships never stay the same. They are either improving or deteriorating, but they never stay static. This is an important law of relationships. We must be aware that in relationships there is no such thing as status quo.

In learning this we become motivated to develop the type of interaction that builds the relationship, instead of destroying. We realize the importance of contact and interaction in our relationships. The question we must ask is, "What type of contact or interaction best builds and strengthens the relationship?"

Fulfilled needs build relationships. Remember the first law of relationships states: "All relationships evolve around personal needs." It is the meeting of those needs that continually builds and strengthens the relationship. Therefore, the goal of any relationship must be the meeting of existing needs.

The truth of this law is one of the reasons Paul told the Philippians, "Do nothing out of selfish ambition or vain conceit, but in humility consider others better than yourselves. Each of you should look not only to your own interests, but also to the interests of others" (Phil. 2:3-4). Focusing on the needs and interests of others is the way to build strong relationships.

The meeting of needs is a full-time job in any personal relationship. We must keep in mind that needs are continually changing. The needs of yesterday are not necessarily the needs of today or tomorrow. We'll discover in later chapters the importance of continually communicating your needs in a relationship. One of the major mistakes we make is to assume that we know the other person's needs or that they know what our needs are. This is especially true in marriage relationships.

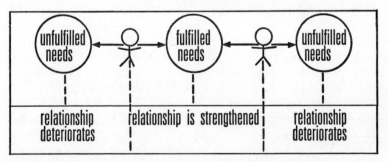

FIGURE 1: The above diagram shows how fulfilled needs help bring people together and strengthen the relationship. However, unfulfilled needs tend to pull them apart and cause the relationship to deteriorate.

The failure to communicate and meet needs is the cause of too many divorces.

As Figure 1 on page 19 illustrates, it is impossible to over-emphasize the importance of meeting needs in a relationship. However, as the figure indicates, each individual in the relationship must be focusing on meeting the needs of the other in order for the relationship to grow and develop. You can never expect to have a healthy and rewarding relationship if only one of the individuals involved is putting forth an effort. We will look at the effects of this in later chapters in the book. At this point we simply need to learn how critical the meeting of needs is to the ongoing development of a relationship.

There are several traps we can fall into when considering the important role of needs in a relationship. First, we may be tempted to play judge and jury in deciding the validity of a so-called need. This is a major mistake. Don't attempt to analyze the validity or importance of a need someone reveals. If you say, "Oh, I don't think that is really a need," you are running the risk of losing the individual's confidence in your sincerity. They may become defensive and stop communicating their needs altogether.

The issue isn't the validity of the need as determined by you; it is are you willing to meet the perceived needs of the other person in the relationship. If the person thinks it is a need then he or she will respond emotionally as if it is a legitimate need. But if you meet only those needs you deem worthy, then you are simply practicing selfishness in one of its most refined and attractive costumes.

In addition, when dealing with needs in the relationship never keep score. If your attitude is, "I'll not meet your need until you meet mine," then there is little hope for a happy, productive relationship. As we will see through the pages of this book, the commitment to meeting needs must be unconditional if we want rewarding relationships.

Unfulfilled needs erode relationships. Show me a person with hurting relationships and I'll show you a person with unfulfilled needs. You never destroy relationships by meeting too many of an individual's needs. However, failure to meet needs in a relationship is the fastest way I know to destroy it.

An unfulfilled need has the same effect on your emotions as a misplaced hammer hit does on your finger—both get your undivided attention. Just as you feel the pain in your finger you feel the hurt and tension generated by an unfulfilled need.

When our needs are not met we begin to focus on ourselves. We withdraw from those who refuse to meet our needs just like we avoid hitting our fingers again with the hammer. No one enjoys the hurt of unfulfilled needs; we do everything in our power to protect ourselves from such hurt. Our posture becomes extremely defensive and protective. Reluctant to run any risks in the relationship that might again open up the wound, we spend more and more time avoiding the issues or people that have created the hurt.

However, unfulfilled needs do not have to spell doom for relationships. Wounds can be healed. Shattered relationships can be restored. Hurts can be turned into happiness. There can be a bright tomorrow, because there is *hope for hurting relationships*.

THE CYCLE OF RELATIONSHIPS

2

Backing out of a crowded parking lot in front of the Denver counseling clinic, a horn honked behind me and I suddenly slammed on my brakes. A woman rolled down her car window and asked if I would join her for a cup of coffee at the restaurant across the street. It was Janice Stone.

As the hostess showed us to our booth Janice said, "I got a call from Charles last week. It's the first time I've talked to him since . . ." she paused to regain her composure then continued, ". . . since he left me in Florida." After two years she still had difficulty saying she was divorced.

I wasn't sure if she expected a response, so I busied myself unfolding a napkin and placing it across my leg. "He asked me to take him back," she said. She nervously ran her finger along the checkered design of the red-and-white plaid tablecloth. I could tell she needed to talk, so after ordering our coffee I waited for her to continue.

With tears rolling down her cheeks, she stared out the window. It was a scene reminiscent of our meeting two years before, only this time there was sunshine instead of cold, blowing snow. "I don't understand," she said after a long silence. "As he was packing his car to leave he told me he didn't love me—that he wasn't sure if he had ever really loved me—and for the first time he had found someone he could talk to, who appreciated and understood him, and made him feel wanted, like a whole man. He said he finally knows what real love is." Expressions of pain, bewilderment, and then anger filled her face as she relived that experience in her mind.

She continued "After moving to Florida, we were both so excited and happy. God had blessed our ministry. We started a family. Things were great." She took a deep breath, aimlessly stirred her cup of untouched coffee, and went on. "Oh, we had a few problems, especially as the ministry got bigger and we both got busier, but I didn't think things were that bad." She looked up from her cup of coffee and said, "How can things be going so good and then get this bad? And if he really loved what's her name—Bridgett—so much why is he wanting to come back to me now?"

Following my meeting with Janice I drove slowly south on Interstate 25 toward Colorado Springs and home. I too was frustrated and angry. Only my anger was directed at myself. Janice's question, *"How can things be going so good and then get this bad?"* kept playing over and over in my mind like a broken record. However, I was thinking about my own life instead of hers. As I topped Monument Hill and gazed upon the magnificent beauty of snow-covered Pikes Peak, tears came to my eyes and again that haunting question rang in my ears and I heard myself repeating it out loud.

I not only lost a marriage but also one of my businesses as a result of the divorce. My family was deeply hurt as well as many within the Christian community. My wife and I had been leaders within the local Christian community, and I had a national ministry of speaking and writing to Christians about management and business. Suddenly my family, business, and credibility within the Christian community was practically destroyed. I could still hardly believe it was true.

I had seen seven counselors during those few months. I was an emotional basket case. At times I felt I couldn't endure another day of the pain, hurt, and hopelessness. Like Janice, a million times I asked myself, "How could things have been going so good and then gotten this bad?" Over the last few years I have had an opportunity to talk with many people who were hurting deeply because of serious relationship problems and I have discovered that most of them have asked that very same question.

The Four Relationship Styles

In order to answer the question we must understand the cycle of relationships. I have observed four types, or styles, of relationships. These are found in organizations as well as marriages and friendships. We will see in later chapters that relationships start out on a positive note but tend to deteriorate as we become more self-centered in our approach to them. As the relationship degenerates we develop a "new style" of relating to those involved. These can be classified into four relationship styles:

▶ Cooperation
▶ Retaliation
▶ Domination
▶ Isolation

In the next four chapters we will take an in-depth look at each of these relationship styles. We will see what causes them to develop, what transpires during each style, how we move from style to style, and the results of moving from cooperation to isolation. However, before we study these closely we need to look at some preliminary information.

The Relationship Cycle

Relationships tend to evolve through a specific, predictable cycle. All relationships start out in a cooperation style. However, as problems begin to develop in the relationship the retaliation style emerges. As the problems worsen the domination style emerges. Then in the final, decaying stages of the relationship the isolation style is predominant. See Figure 2.

Just like nature, the relationship cycle moves through a series of ever-dissolving seasons. However, as diagramed in Figure 3 on page 27, the difference between the four seasons and the four relationship styles is that at any point along the decaying process a relationship can be restored to cooperation. Seasons move in a sequential cycle, but relationships need not be condemned to an inevitable end.

It is much easier to restore a relationship to cooperation from retaliation than when it has evolved into isolation. The

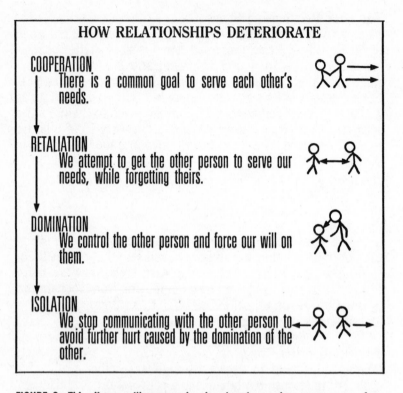

HOW RELATIONSHIPS DETERIORATE

COOPERATION
There is a common goal to serve each other's needs.

RETALIATION
We attempt to get the other person to serve our needs, while forgetting theirs.

DOMINATION
We control the other person and force our will on them.

ISOLATION
We stop communicating with the other person to avoid further hurt caused by the domination of the other.

FIGURE 2: This diagram illustrates the deteriorating cycle as one moves from the cooperation style toward the isolation style of relationships.

longer the restoration process is delayed the harder it is to return to a cooperation style and the greater the risk that the relationship will be terminated. In fact, most every couple that enters the divorce courts is in an isolation relationship style. At least one of the individuals in the marriage relationship has concluded the situation is hopeless and has given up on it.

How Changing Needs Influence Relationships

Many people ask the question, "Why do relationships move from being productive and rewarding through the relationship

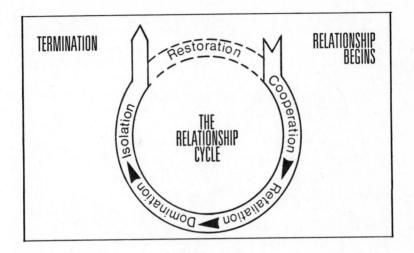

FIGURE 3: The above diagram shows the importance of the restoration process in maintaining a healthy and rewarding cooperation relationship style.

cycle and end in termination of the relationship?" There are many reasons; however, I believe there are five frequent failures:

▶ The wrong objective for entering the relationship
▶ Failure to meet changing needs
▶ Changing goals and interests
▶ Failure to communicate needs, goals, and interests
▶ Failure to make the relationship a priority

The wrong objective for entering the relationship. In chapter 1 we pointed out that relationships evolve around personal needs and that fulfilled needs build relationships, whereas unfulfilled needs erode them. People form relationships in order to have their needs met. And therein lies the problem for some people. If you form a relationship simply to get your own needs met, but aren't willing to meet the needs of the other person or people, that relationship is doomed for failure.

Unfortunately many people are so self-centered that their

only objective for forming a relationship is to get their own needs met. They are unwilling to spend the time and energy it takes to meet the needs of the other person. Such people, when confronted, usually accuse others of being what they are—selfish.

For example, Bill, my next-door neighbor, drives to Denver every day to work, as do several other people in my neighborhood. In order to save money on his commuting Bill organized a car pool with the others. There were four people in the pool and each was to take his turn to drive for a week.

Everything was working fine until Doug's turn to drive. Before joining the pool Doug, to save fuel, had been driving his "Volkswagen Bug" to work, instead of his larger family car. However, when it came his turn to drive he would have had to drive the larger car in order to have enough room for four people and their belongings. This was going to cost Doug more money for fuel, so after riding three weeks free in the car pool he dropped out when it came his turn. Saying his family car needed some work done, he informed the others that he would be unable to continue participating in the pool.

Bill confronted Doug, saying that he felt he should pay each of the drivers something for the weeks he rode free. Doug became very angry at Bill and accused him of just trying to make money on the car pool. He said he had been perfectly happy driving his own car to work and only joined the pool because he knew they were having trouble finding a fourth person to participate.

Bill told me, "You know, at first he almost had me feeling like a heel until I realized what he was doing. He was just trying to cover up his own greed and realized he had found three suckers who would give him a free ride to work for a while."

Unfortunately there are all too many people like Doug. They are out to get all they can get from a relationship, but when it comes their turn to give back they are ready to terminate it. People in such relationships have two choices. They can allow the person to take advantage of them or they can confront the individual. If you say nothing to such people you are doing yourself and them a disservice. You will never have a rewarding relationship if your needs aren't being met. And if you say nothing you are only giving license to the individual to keep practicing selfishness and encouraging its continuance in other relationships. However, confrontation with such people, as in the previous example, often leads to the termination of the relationship.

We need to remember that there are basically two kinds of relationships, binding and casual. Binding relationships include marriages, relationships between parents and children, ones with relatives and in-laws, those with bosses and employees, and all other relationships that one considers permanent and of long-term lasting value. A casual relationship consists of those with acquaintances, neighbors who aren't close friends, and other nonbinding relationships.

We need to mention these two types of relationships because our obligations to those we consider binding are much greater (or should be) than those we would consider as casual. Therefore, our response to a person in a binding relationship who refuses to meet our need should be different than our reaction to such a situation in a casual relationship. Binding relationships are more permanent in nature and there are very few instances in which we could justify terminating the relationship. However, that is not always true in the case of casual relationships.

Failure to meet changing needs. Regardless of whether it is a personal or professional relationship, the needs within it are continually changing. Failure to meet changing needs is one of the major causes of breakdown from cooperation toward isolation.

During one of my conversations with Janice Stone, she admitted that toward the end of her marriage with Charles neither one of them was effectively meeting the other one's needs. "When we first moved to Florida, Charles thought it was a great idea for me to conduct workshops and speak at women's retreats," she said. "In fact, he insisted on it. He thought it made us more of a team. And it was his idea for me to host a local Christian radio program. He said it would broaden our service to the whole community and help promote our church."

"What happened?" I asked, wondering if I had a right to inquire. "We both got so busy," she explained. "After a while both of our jobs were taking up so much time that we only saw each other in passing on the way to the next meeting, appointment, or speaking engagement.

"We realized we needed to make some changes and on several occasions he asked me to drop the talk show and cut back on the out of town speaking engagements, but I felt he was just getting jealous because my ministry was getting to be as big as his." She shook her head and dropped her eyes to the floor, feeling the pangs of guilt once more. "He kept saying he needed me home more, but I honestly thought he was just jealous of my work."

Janice and Charles Stone were not sensitive to one another's changing needs. They were talented and gifted people who rendered a great service to the Christian community. However, they were no longer meeting the changing needs in their relationship. And as we will see clearly in future chapters, once we stop meeting the changing needs of a relationship, no matter how strong that relationship might have been in the past, we are headed away from cooperation and have begun that painful trip down the road to isolation and eventually termination.

We must never assume that because a relationship is good today that it will always stay that way. A relationship is rewarding only as we meet the needs of one another. Never be deceived into thinking that a good relationship could never be destroyed. Relationships remain strong and rewarding only as long as the people in them are effectively meeting one another's changing needs. The needs of tomorrow will likely be a lot different from those of today.

In 1973 I was on the verge of getting a divorce. However, I made a strong commitment to the relationship, worked hard for several years to rebuild my marriage, and thought that everything was going great. In fact, my wife and I used to travel around the country putting on marriage seminars. I thought my marriage could never be destroyed. However, we both got busy. I had three businesses. My wife had a full-time career. We began to take each other for granted. We assumed we knew each other's needs and neglected to work at serving one another. We slowly drifted apart. The old hurts and wounds were reopened. The old communication barriers were rebuilt. And over a period of time the relationship that once had been strong and healthy crumbled from within and was destroyed.

If it could happen to me, it could also happen to you—no matter how secure you feel—if you fail to continue meeting the changing needs within the relationship.

Changing goals and interests. Just as needs change within a relationship, so do goals and interests. In order to maintain an ongoing cooperation style relationship, those involved must make sure their goals and interests remain compatible. They don't always have to remain the same; however, they must not conflict with one another.

Rick and Betty Dobson used to live next door. They had two girls in grade school. Rick was an electronics engineer, and Betty stayed home and took care of the household responsibilities. Betty decided she would like to move into a larger home and agreed to get a paying job in order to help make the larger house payments. Betty went to work as an interior decorator and before long decided to start her own design business.

Rick did not want her to start the business because of the increased financial burden; however, he went along with Betty's desire, and they both signed a note to help finance Betty's newfound business. Betty was gone a lot working with clients, and since Rick knew nothing about interior design he stayed as far away as possible.

However, in order to fill up his time while Betty was working, Rick joined a local health club where he soon met two people who were members of a mountain climbing club. Since he loved the outdoors it didn't take long for them to talk Rick into joining. He asked Betty to join with him, but her new business schedule prevented her.

Over a period of time both Rick and Betty developed radically different goals and interests. Betty's business became very successful, but it required almost all of her time. On the other hand, Rick became more involved on weekends and during the evenings with the mountain climbing club. Over an extended period of time Rick and Betty developed different friends, interests, and lifestyles.

I wasn't surprised when Rick called me one day and told me he and Betty had filed for divorce. "We both decided we had outgrown each other and needed to move on to new and different things," Rick said rather matter-of-factly, like getting a divorce was no different than trading the old car in on a new one. "We just don't have things in common anymore. She's seeing some doctor down at the hospital and I've been dating one of the members of the mountain climbing club, so I guess it's time to swim down different streams," he concluded.

I wasn't surprised they were getting a divorce. I had been watching them steadily drift apart. However, I was surprised at how indifferent he was about the whole thing. It is amazing what happens when people in a relationship allow such conflicting goals and interests to develop.

Rick and Betty had become total strangers living under the same roof. They allowed their changing goals and interests to destroy what had once been a healthy and happy marriage.

To maintain a cooperation style relationship, that continually meets the needs of those involved, mutually compatible goals and interests that help build up one another must be developed. Any lesser compromise will drive those involved further and further apart.

Failure to communicate needs, goals, and interests. In order to meet changing needs and maintain compatible interests, it is necessary to communicate in those areas of the relationship. You can't meet new and changing needs if you don't know they exist. You can't maintain mutual goals unless you are willing to discuss their impact and influence on the relationship.

This should seem obvious. However, I have observed that it is frequently the obvious that is most often the last to receive attention, or is overlooked altogether. Therefore, I can't over-emphasize the need for ongoing communication concerning the maturing changes in a relationship. Many relationships, including my own marriage, could have been saved if those involved would have taken the time to effectively communicate in these very critical areas.

Failure to make the relationship a priority. What do I mean by that? Most people would say their relationships are a priority—especially their binding relationships. However, it isn't enough to simply *say* a relationship has high priority.

The mark of how important something is to us is measured by the amount of time we invest in it. Unfortunately, it took me a long time to learn that. I used to think I could show my family their importance by spending money on them. I bought my wife a new home, furniture, cars, clothes, and took her out to eat several times a week. But, during the final years of our marriage I rarely spent quality time with either my wife or children. I was too busy making money for them to give them my time also.

If you want to discover a person's priorities look at how time is spent, not money. Money can always be replaced, but time never can. Time represents your life. It is a most prized possession and we invest it in our most important priorities. The more time we give to something the higher it is on our priority list. The less time we invest in something the lower it is.

Using time as a measuring stick, I realize that for years my business must have been more important to me than my family. It is very hard to admit that, even now. I would have vigorously denied it a few years ago and told you I was making money so I could buy nice things for my family. However, my family didn't want the nice things nearly as much as they wanted me.

My priorities were out of order. I had become deceived into

thinking that things were what made people happy and rela-tionships strong. I realize now that isn't true. People are what make relationships strong, not things. Material objects can never meet the deep interpersonal needs of a relationship. Only people spending time with people can meet those needs.

So if your relationships are important to you, or if you want to make them your top priority, then prove it by giving of your time to make them productive. Because it's only as you give of your time to the relationship that you really give yourself to another person.

God's Concern for Your Relationships

Many people have strange ideas about God and His interest in the affairs of humanity. Some people think God lives far away and is totally detached and uninterested in the affairs of Earth. Others don't even believe God exists. Still others believe God is so busy with the maintenance of the universe that He certainly couldn't have time to be bothered with the petty problems of personal relationships.

I have to admit that from time to time I have questioned all of the above issues concerning God. In my darkest hours of despair, hurt, and pain I have found myself wondering about—yes, even questioning—the existence of God. I have been tempted to believe He doesn't really care about me and my problems. However, I have discovered that He does care. He is available to help. He does have answers.

My problem hasn't been knowing the answer, it has been a willingness to apply the relationship principles that God has ordained for His creation. I have discovered that the principles presented in the Bible work better than any modern-day the-ory or belief on satisfying relationships. In fact, I have discov-ered that many of the ideas offered by modern-day counselors do more to destroy relationships than build them because their thinking is built around the promotion and pacification of self. This deification of self destroys relationships instead of building them.

Six of the Ten Commandments deal with our relationship to

one another while the other four deal with our relationship to God. All of them deal with relationships; that should tell us something about God's interest in our interpersonal dynamics with Him and with one another.

The Bible is the greatest textbook ever written to guide us in living a full and happy life marked by meaningful relationships. If we can learn to apply the interpersonal principles written on its pages, we can avoid a great deal of hurt, pain, and anxiety in all of our various relationships.

THE COOPERATION RELATIONSHIP STYLE

3

All relationships tend to begin in a cooperation style. Those involved begin the relationship with the intent of meeting one another's needs. For example, think back on your first day at work on a new job. You went to work committed to serve the needs of the company. If you are married think back to your wedding day. It was one of the happiest days of your life. You and your mate were committed to serving one another's needs. You began the relationship in a cooperation style.

If you've never been married think back to your first serious relationship. Your goal was to act the right way, impress your boy or girl friend, and do the things that made them happy. Think about the first time you met your friend's parents. Your goal was to make a good impression and please them. We all tend to start relationships committed to meeting and serving the needs of those involved.

The Cooperation Style Is Unique
As figure 4 on page 38 illustrates, the cooperation style is unique in that it is the only type of relationship that focuses on serving others. All of the other styles focus on getting others to serve us. People committed to a cooperation style relationship say, "I will serve your needs." When everyone focuses on serving each other's needs then needs are being met. It is important to realize that *to have a cooperation relationship, each person involved must be committed to serving the other.* That is the only way needs can continually be met.

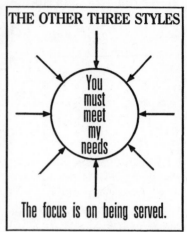

FIGURE 4: The cooperation relationship's focus differs widely from the other three styles.

The Bible is filled with principles on developing and maintaining rewarding relationships. Jesus said, "In everything do to others what you would have them do to you" (Matt. 7:12). And what is it we would have others do to us? Meet our needs. Therefore, we are to treat others the way we want to be treated in a relationship. If we do, all needs in the relationship will be met. Also, in Romans 15:2 we are told, "Each of us should please his neighbor for his good, to build him up."

These two verses along with Philippians 2:3-4 lay the foundation for the cooperation style relationship. If each of us pleases our neighbor then we all will have our needs met. That is the purpose of a cooperation style relationship.

The Profile of the Cooperation Relationship
The cooperation relationship style consists of the following characteristics:
▶ A strong commitment to meet the needs of the other person
▶ De-emphasizing of self

▶ Strong mutual trust and respect
▶ The mutual encouragement of creativity and decision-making
▶ Joint problem solving
▶ A willingness to be transparent
▶ A willingness to forgive and forget mistakes
▶ A strong emphasis on teamwork

A strong commitment to meet the needs of the other person. The cooperation relationship style is built on such a commitment. This commitment to serve the other must be practiced by all involved in order to develop and maintain a cooperation relationship.

One of the best ways to get your needs met is to first be willing to meet the needs of others. I have seen that demonstrated in my own life and the Bible effectively illustrates the principle in 1 Kings. This chapter tells the story of Rehoboam, Solomon's son, becoming king after the death of his father. The young king asked the elders who had served under his father how he should lead the people. Notice their answer: "If today you will be a servant to these people and serve them and give them a favorable answer, they will always be your servants" (1 Kings 12:7).

This verse gives us a very important principle for relationships. It tells us that when we serve others they will serve us in return.

For example, Milton Evans, one of my neighbors, was not a very friendly man. I had waved to him on the street and tried to talk to him on occasion, but he seemed very reserved and not interested in being friends.

Last Thanksgiving Day we had a big snowstorm in the mountains of Colorado where I live. Milton couldn't get his car out of the snowdrift blocking his driveway. He was very upset because he and his wife, Thelma, were late to Thanksgiving dinner at their daughter's home across town.

I saw Milton trying to tunnel out of a large snowdrift and realized, unless he had help, he would be spending his day shoveling instead of with his daughter. And even if he got out of the driveway I wasn't sure he could make it to his daughter's place midst the two foot snowdrifts in the street.

I loaned Milton and Thelma my four-wheel drive pickup and told them I would help shovel their car out after the storm was over. They were very grateful and tried to pay me for the use of my pickup. When I refused payment Milton said, "Well, Myron, I'll pay you back somehow. You're being awfully kind to us, and we're not going to let you do this for nothing."

Late that evening Milton brought my pickup back and handed me a large box of fresh oysters in the shell and a box of large frozen shrimp. Milton owned a wholesale seafood business. He said, "We have more of this stuff around the house than we can ever use, so we thought you might like some." I thanked him for the seafood and he said, "We'd like you to come over for dinner some evening. We need to get better acquainted with our neighbors."

I couldn't believe how Milton had changed. He seemed to be going out of his way to become a friend. However, before I had helped him he had been very cold and distant toward me.

The next time I drove my pickup I discovered that Milton had filled it with fuel even though he had only driven it about five miles. To this day he and his wife still mention how grateful they were for helping them out during the Thanksgiving Day snowstorm. We have become good friends and they still do things to show their appreciation for helping them during their time of need.

Cooperation relationships are built on a commitment to serve others within the relationship. And as 1 Kings 12:7 illustrates, when we serve others they tend to want to serve us in return. Milton and Thelma certainly demonstrated to me the principle of that verse.

De-emphasizing of self. In a cooperation relationship we not only are committed to meeting other's needs, but we de-emphasize self. That doesn't mean that we ignore our own needs and concerns. We certainly must communicate them. However, our first priority is serving "the other" in the relationship. We must never serve simply as a means of manipulating others to serve us. Such false servitude is easily exposed.

When I saw Milton snowbound in his own driveway I didn't think, "Ah, here is an opportunity to serve him so he will have to serve me!" I simply saw a man in need and met it, expecting nothing in return. In a cooperation relationship our goal is to meet the needs of others instead of trying to have our own needs met. In other words, there are no strings attached to our service and actions. We sincerely seek to meet the needs of others. We promote others and deemphasize self.

The beauty of the cooperation relationship style is that we serve others freely and openly, requiring nothing in return. However, as we do we will discover a great Old Testament truth. "One man gives freely, yet gains even more; another withholds unduly, but comes to poverty. A generous man will prosper; he who refreshes others will himself be refreshed" (Prov. 11:24-25).

This passage contains some great truths and principles that are applicable to our relationships. As we freely serve the needs of others our needs are met in return; however, when we fail to meet others' needs we soon discover that our own needs are going unfulfilled.

Another feature of the cooperation relationship style is that those involved emphasize meeting the other person's needs. In that way needs within the relationship are continually being met. However, as soon as self is promoted instead of others, the relationship will begin to deteriorate.

Strong mutual trust and respect. Strong mutual trust and respect occurs in a cooperation relationship when people focus on meeting one another's needs. Trust and respect must be *earned,* it is never produced upon demand. Trust and respect is earned through the meeting of needs. We trust and respect those people who continually meet our needs.

If you have to demand trust and respect in a relationship you can be assured you haven't earned it. People in a cooperation relationship don't trust one another because it is expected, but because they are serving one another by meeting the existing needs. It is easy to trust people who are consistently meeting your needs. But no amount of demanding will acquire it.

An important distinction must be made; it is possible to be doing lots of things for people, but not really be meeting their needs. I was a classic example of that prior to my divorce. I was so busy doing things for my family that I didn't meet their needs.

I spent all of my time making money so I could buy my family things, but I wasn't meeting their needs. As a result my wife started mistrusting my motives. She thought the business had become more important to me than my family. I was hurt and angry because I thought my family didn't appreciate all I was doing for them. As a result we lost respect for one another. Why? Because I was doing lots of things for my family, but not the things that met their needs.

This is a very common trap for families today. We live in a busy, rapid-paced society. In many homes both the husband and wife work. They do so thinking it will meet more of the family's needs. However, in many instances they discover, sometimes too late, that they have been busy doing things for one another, and buying things for one another, but not meeting the important family needs.

Today's highly materialistic society has deceived many of us into thinking that all needs can be met by *things*. We tend to believe that things are the key to our happiness and therefore they sometimes become the focal point of our relationships. However, our most important people needs can only be met as we give ourselves to one another. The people in our relationships need our undivided attention, understanding, empathy, and smiles much more than they need things. Trust and respect come as a result of giving ourselves to others, not from the "things" we can buy each other.

Mutual encouragement of creativity and decision-making. The cooperation relationship not only focuses on meeting needs, it also emphasizes the mutual utilization of creativity and decision-making. That is one of the reasons this type of relationship is so productive. Each person in the relationship works at drawing out and promoting the creativity and potential of the other.

Janice Stone had indicated that the first 10 years in Florida were the happiest time of her life. One of the reasons was Charles' continual encouragement to use her creativity. He promoted her gifts, abilities, and creativity. It allowed Janice to make decisions, use her skills, and contribute to the ministry and their relationship.

Janice was made to feel needed and that she was making a very important contribution. She was encouraged to become involved in activities that made her an important part of her marriage relationship with Charles and their joint ministry. The ministry became "theirs," not just "his."

In a cooperation relationship there is a feeling of mutual ownership of the plans, projects, and accomplishments because there is mutual input of creativity and decision-making. Those in the relationship are considered equals. There is equal and mutual respect for ideas and input. That does not mean that the group or relationship is without a leader. However, it is shared leadership. The individuals within the relationship are encouraged to assume leadership in the areas where they are gifted.

Such mutual encouragement of creativity means that the individual best suited for a certain activity will be given the opportunity to perform those functions. This allows people the opportunity to work in their area of strength and helps increase the overall productivity within the relationship.

Unfortunately, in relationship styles other than cooperation, people often feel threatened if another person is given an opportunity to excel in areas where they do not feel as competent. As a result, excessive competition often develops within those relationships barring individuals from actively participating in mutual decisions within the relationship.

That is apparently what happened in Janice and Charles Stone's relationship. Toward the end of their relationship she felt he was jealous of her accomplishments and tried to get her to curtail her activities. People in cooperation relationships guard against such jealousy because they know it quickly destroys the environment.

The strengths of individuals are what attract us to them. However, in marriage relationships, too often it is the strengths we saw initially that become the areas around which conflict develops.

During a conversation with Janice Stone she said, "One of the things that attracted me to Charles was his great love for people and ability to relate to them. However, once we were married our biggest fights centered around his need to have people around him all the time. I felt like I was always competing for Charles' time."

To develop and maintain a cooperation relationship we must be willing to overlook people's weaknesses and allow them to capitalize on their strengths. We must be willing to promote those strengths and encourage people to be as creative as possible in developing and utilizing them. In order to do so we must avoid feeling threatened by the other person's gifts.

To avoid feeling threatened by a person's abilities in a relationship, one must focus on how those talents can make the best contribution within the relationship as well as outside it. Within many relationships, especially marriage, individuals are forced to use their abilities outside of it since there isn't a proper opportunity within the relationship.

For example, I met Jack and Edna Long while conducting a management seminar in Anchorage, Alaska. Jack is a pilot for a mission organization and Edna is a CPA and works for an accounting firm. When I met them they were having serious relationship problems centering around money. Jack felt that as the leader of the home he should be in charge of the finances. Although he was a great pilot, he was not very good at keeping track of the family finances.

Edna had insisted they attend the seminar in hopes Jack could learn to better manage their finances. After the seminar was over they both approached me and during the conversation that followed Edna said, "I don't have a problem with Jack being in charge of the finances, but it is embarrassing when we continually have bounced checks and overdrafts at the bank because he can't keep the records straight."

Jack readily agreed, but someone had told him that it was his Christian duty to manage the finances, even though he hated it. However, by the end of our conversation they both agreed that it only made sense for Edna to keep the financial books because she was trained in accounting, enjoyed working with figures, and had the time and interest to devote to the job.

One of the main objectives of the cooperation relationship style is to determine the talents and interests of those within the relationship and determine how their concerns can best be utilized within the relationship, as well as outside it. And as you do so, like Jack and Edna, you will discover the relationship will not only improve, but people will be given an opportunity to do those things they do best.

Joint problem-solving. All relationships experience problems from time to time. However, in a cooperation style relationship problems are solved jointly. Everyone involved in the relationship is encouraged to provide input into developing a solution. This is one of the ways individuals have an opportunity to use their creativity and gifts.

All too often one person in a relationship tends to emerge as the problem solver and decision maker. When this occurs others are stifled in the use of their own skills.

When everyone is involved in solving problems it makes it easier to find solutions. Within the cooperation style the emphasis is on how each individual can contribute to the solution. In that way everyone develops a sense of ownership for the problem and its solution.

A willingness to be transparent. It is imperative that people in cooperation relationships be transparent with one another. If you are going to meet each other's needs you must first know what those needs are, no matter how personal.

You must be willing, and have the freedom, to express how you really think and feel. Encourage one another to share differences, even where there is strong disagreement. This is an important key to the cooperation relationship style to which we will devote a chapter later in the book.

A willingness to forgive and forget mistakes. Cooperation style relationships are marked by a willingness to forgive and forget mistakes. Without forgiveness one is on the road to deteriorating relationships. Unfortunately, most of us have problems with both forgiving and forgetting.

One day Peter came to Jesus asking Him how many times he should be required to forgive and suggested that he thought seven times should be plenty. However, notice how Jesus answered him. "I tell you, not seven times, but seventy-seven times" (Matt. 18:22).

Jesus was teaching a very important principle of relationships in that statement. He was telling us we should keep no records of forgiving people. We should not have a limit on our forgiveness. This is a key ingredient to maintaining a healthy relationship.

In 1 Corinthians 13:5 we learn that love "keeps no record of wrongs." That must be the case if we are to practice a cooperation style. Because we are human all of us are guilty of hurting others in our relationships. However, we should never be guilty of not forgiving a person who wrongs us.

When we stop forgiving we are no longer in a cooperation relationship type. Failure to forgive leads to the next step to get even. At that point, as we will see later, we have crossed the line into a retaliation style relationship.

It is not enough to forgive when someone in a relationship wrongs you, you must also be willing to forget. Forgiving and forgetting go hand in hand. You must first forgive an offense before you can forget it. As long as you are harboring ill feelings toward someone it is impossible to forget and put the situation behind you. Until you forgive and forget you run the risk of destroying a cooperation relationship.

People in a cooperation relationship never wait for the other person to say, "I'm sorry," even if they were not the one causing the problem. They are willing to go to the other person at the first sign of a problem and attempt to resolve it.

Jesus Christ taught this principle when He said, "If you are offering your gift at the altar and there remember that your brother has something against you, leave your gift there in front of the altar. First go and be reconciled to your brother; then come and offer your gift" (Matt. 5:23-24).

The passage points out that even though you are not the one with the problem, you are the one who is to initiate the reconciliation process. This is often hard to do because we feel the person who has wronged us should begin the reconciliation. But to maintain the cooperation relationship style we must be willing to swallow our pride and initiate, even when the other person is in the wrong.

A strong emphasis on team work. People in a cooperation style relationship are working together as a team, not as separate individuals seeking their own independent goals. They have team goals and are working together to achieve them. Teamwork plays an important role. Later in the book we will devote a chapter to the development of effective team work.

It Will Take Lots of Hard Work
There are no shortcuts to developing and maintaining a cooperation style relationship. It takes continual work, effort, and commitment. You never arrive at the perfect relationship. There are always areas that need improvement. However, you can develop and maintain a cooperation relationship style.

In an earlier chapter we said that relationships are constantly changing. They are either improving or deteriorating. Never forget that *it is much easier to maintain a good relationship than it is to repair a bad one.* So make a strong commitment to maintaining a good relationship and keep working at it because it is the best investment you can make.

The Role Commitment Plays
Commitment alone will not produce a positive and rewarding relationship. You must be committed to building and maintaining a good relationship, not just committed to the relationship. My aunt and uncle lived together until they died.

They were committed to the relationship. They never left each other. They were never unfaithful. However, they had a miserable life together. They fought continually. I never saw them show affection toward one another. They continually criticized one another.

They were not only miserable together, but they made everyone else miserable who was around them. *But they never left each other!* They lived together in the same house until they died. Their problem was that they were only committed to the staying together, but they were not committed to having a *good* relationship.

Christians must be committed to developing rewarding relationships. I believe my aunt and uncle's situation was as sad as if they had gotten a divorce. They certainly were not applying biblical principles in their marriage relationship. In fact, they violated almost every principle of marriage listed in the Bible.

Be committed to true love. What is true love? Our songs long for it, our books try to describe it, our movies attempt to depict it, but how many of us really know what love is? We talk about falling in and out of love. We all need love. How would you define love? Your definition of love will have a great impact on your relationships with others.

According to 1 Corinthians 13:4-8 love is an action. Notice the adjectives the passage uses to define love: "Love is patient, love is kind. It does not envy, it does not boast, it is not proud. It is not rude, it is not self-seeking, it is not easily angered, it keeps no record of wrongs. Love does not delight in evil but rejoices with the truth. It always protects, always trusts, always hopes, always perseveres. Love never fails."

This is true love in action. This is what we need in our relationships. Unfortunately, most people today want to define love as a feeling. A commitment is made to the feeling, and when the feeling is gone the commitment is over. People move on, looking for the feeling again with someone else.

Make a commitment in your life to apply the actions described in the 1 Corinthians 13 passage. You will develop strong feelings of love as well. When dealing with true love, the action comes first followed later by the feeling. True love is action. It is treating others the way you want to be treated. As you do, you will develop the emotional attachment toward that individual as well.

We are living in a time in which relational problems are all around us. Even the Christian community, with its traditionally stable homes, is reeling from the shock waves of broken marriages and relationship crises within the lives of respected Christian leaders.

Since my own devastating experience with divorce I am even more aware of the need for commitment to strong relationships. I can understand more fully why God says He hates divorce. I also hate divorce. More now than ever because I have experienced its destructive path in all areas of my life.

Chapter Summary

We have looked at the cooperation style relationship and how it may be developed and maintained. It is a highly rewarding and beneficial relationship style for all those who commit to it and apply its principles. And we have seen it is the type of relationship that God wants for us.

However, we are all human. We all make mistakes. From time to time we fail. And no matter how committed you are to a cooperation style relationship, from time to time you will find yourself slowly moving away from it.

The next three chapters focus on the results of losing a grip on the cooperation relationship style. We will see how we develop habits, attitudes, and actions that cause us to stop focusing on the needs of others. We will see the end result of selfishness and how it can use the control of individuals to finally destroy relationships.

As you read these chapters look for your own style. Try to determine where you are in your relationships with others. Be honest with yourself. Determine what you must do to develop and maintain a strong cooperation style relationship. Use that information to make your relationships more rewarding both for yourself and for your significant others.

THE RETALIATION RELATIONSHIP STYLE

4

I don't know how many times the phone rang before I dragged myself away from my dreams to answer it. As I reached for the phone I strained my half-open, out-of-focus eyes to read my wristwatch. It was 3:30 in the morning!

Even though it put up a good fight, I finally forced my brain awake in time to hear someone saying over the phone, "I'm so sorry to call you this time of morning. Please forgive me, but I just had to talk to someone and my counselor is out of town." It was Janice Stone. I couldn't imagine why she would be calling me this time of night.

I didn't have to wait long to find out why she had called. For the next hour I listened as she vented her anger, fear, and frustration. Her son, David, had arrived a few weeks earlier from her parents where he had been staying.

The first few days he had been a model child. He had volunteered to do the dishes. He cleaned his room every day without being reminded and he played all his younger sister's games with her. "Everything was going great until he asked to live with his dad and I refused. Now he's acting horrible!" Janice said with a hint of panic in her voice.

Since Janice had refused to let David live with his father he had been fighting with his younger sister continually. He had also gotten in trouble with the kids across the street, cut her cousin's new drapes with a pair of scissors, pulled the arms off his sister's doll, and if that wasn't enough, one of the clerks at the grocery store had caught him stealing a candy bar while Janice was shopping.

When I asked her what she was doing in the way of discipline she said frantically, "Every time I discipline him he tries to hit me and demands to live with his dad. He tells me I hate him and that he's going to run away if I don't let him go." She was almost in tears as she continued, "We had a bad argument tonight. And that's why I called you. I made him go to his room early. A few minutes ago I went to check on him and he was putting clothes in his suitcase. He is going to run away if I don't let him go to his father. I don't know what to do!"

I learned that for the past several months Charles had been writing and calling David at his grandparents'. He promised to make arrangements with Janice for David to come and live with his dad at the end of the summer. I asked Janice if Charles had talked to her about it and she said, "Yes, he's called me several times. But I'm not about to let my son go there and live with Charles and that horrible woman! I want David brought up decently. They'd ruin him!"

When I asked her what Charles thought about it all she said, "He's threatening to take me to court. He says he'll win in court because he has a very good job. When the court sees that we're living with relatives, seeing a counselor, and not making much money, they will give him custody of David."

Fear and desperation were evident in her voice as she continued, "What should I do? We were getting along fine until he started begging me to live with his dad. I just don't understand why David is acting so bad!"

David was acting out what I call a "retaliation relationship style." He was lashing out at those around him because he felt he had an unfulfilled need. He launched a struggle for control in his relationship with his mother. And he was doing everything in his power to win that struggle so he could get what he wanted.

We may look at David's actions and say that he was just spoiled and needed the strong hand of discipline. However, all of us from time to time act like David in our relationships with others. When we do we are entangled in the clutches of a retaliation relationship style.

Why Retaliation Relationships Develop

The retaliation relationship style is the first step away from cooperation. It usually happens unconsciously at first. A need develops, and for a moment we change our focus from serving the needs of others to getting others to serve our need. In the beginning the shift is so subtle that we aren't aware what is happening. For a period of time we tend to fluctuate back and forth between cooperation and retaliation, each time placing more emphasis on getting our needs met while neglecting the needs of others.

The retaliation relationship style *always* develops as a result of a decision to put our needs ahead of others. Though we have been operating in a cooperation style relationship, we now decide our needs should take precedence over others. This happens for a variety of reasons as shown below:

▶ We conclude our needs are more important than those of others.

▶ We feel a "right" to be served instead of continuing to serve.

▶ We conclude the other person will no longer voluntarily meet our needs.

Let's consider each of these reasons. As we examine them evaluate how often you have found yourself arriving at the same conclusions. Try to determine how you acted toward others in the relationship as a result.

We conclude our needs are more important than those of others. In a cooperation relationship we aren't concerned with evaluating whose needs are more important. Each person in the relationship is committed to meeting the needs of the other. However, as soon as we start judging which needs are important in the relationship we begin to close the door on cooperation and move toward a retaliation relationship. At that point we invite our own prejudices to begin controlling the relationship. In most instances our self-centered nature is going to choose our own needs and desires over those of others. Naturally we can justify this. But the Bible points out, "We can always 'prove' that we are right, but is the Lord convinced?" (Prov. 16:2, TLB)

Most of us have little problem convincing ourselves that we "deserve" to have our needs met first. Our "me first" society is a direct reflection of our individual attitudes and feelings about self. Human nature always tends to promote self over others. It is this strong temptation to exalt self that slowly chips away at the cooperation style and lays the foundation for an isolation relationship.

The self's unsatisfiable appetite to be served causes people to feel justified in insisting that their needs be met first or at the expense of others.

We feel a "right" to be served instead of continuing to serve. Feeling a right to be served instead of serving is a second cause for moving away from cooperation into retaliation. When we demand the right to be served it is easy to justify our self-centered actions and neglect of the other person's needs.

I first met Ed and Jaylene Parker while enrolling in graduate school. We were waiting in the business office to pay our bill. We struck up a conversation and soon discovered that we would be taking several classes together.

For the past five years the Parkers had been teaching in a Kansas City high school. They had saved their money to go to school full-time instead of taking only a few summer classes and dragging their master's degrees over several years. They didn't have children and were planning to live in married student housing.

Over the next year and a half I became good friends with Ed and Jaylene. We had several classes together and spent a lot of time studying and doing research in the library. One day, toward the end of graduate school, I met Ed and Jaylene in the student union to hear about a great job she had been offered.

Jaylene was a very attractive, self-confident, and out-going person. That day she was all smiles as we found a corner table. I soon learned the reason for Jaylene's smiles and the deep frown that covered Ed's face. Jaylene had been offered a job in the marketing department of a large California corporation, with a starting salary of twice what she had last been making as a teacher.

The school district where Ed had taught promised him a job as a principal if he would return to the district after completing his master's degree. Both Ed and Jaylene had grown up in Kansas City and his elderly mother lived only a few blocks from the school where he would be working. It was obvious that there was much tension over the job offer.

"Ed is mad at me because I want to take this job," Jaylene said as she handed me a copy of the job description. "This is the opportunity of a lifetime and I know Ed could find a teaching position or some kind of job there." Ed interrupted. "That's the problem!" he said, almost yelling in Jaylene's face. "All you're doing is thinking about yourself! What about me and my career! I've waited five years to get a job in school administration and now you want us to move off to California because you've been offered some glamour job. And what about Mom? Whose going to take care of her while we're 2,000 miles away letting you play corporate career girl?"

For the next hour I listened to a husband and wife angrily argue about their future, each thinking the other was wrong. Ed felt they should stay in Kansas City, but Jaylene saw this as a great opportunity to start a new life. She had never liked the Midwest, even though she had lived there all her life. She saw the job as a great challenge with unlimited opportunity and felt Ed was being selfish and unfair in wanting to stay in Kansas City.

"They are looking for bright, energetic young people with the capability and drive to move up in the corporation," Jaylene said as she put the job description back in her briefcase. "And they must think I have that potential, because they offered me the job after interviewing over 100 people for the position!" She had an almost defiant look on her face as she continued. "I don't think it's fair for Ed to try and stop me from taking this job. I think I have just as much right to a satisfying career as he does, and it's obvious I have the potential of making a lot more money than he ever will."

Both Ed and Jaylene felt they had a right to have their needs met in the situation. Each of them thought their particular need was more important than the other's. As we will see later in this chapter, such conclusions usually lead people into a retaliation relationship style.

We conclude the other person will no longer voluntarily meet our needs. This usually causes people to decide to take things into their own hands to get their needs met. At that point we have stopped trusting others, and have convinced ourselves that they are more committed to their needs than to ours. It then becomes necessary to convince others to meet our needs, even if it means "forcing" them to do so.

David came to this conclusion at the beginning of this chapter. He acted that way toward his mother. He concluded Janice would never voluntarily meet his perceived need and therefore he took aggressive action to get his need met. He was on his way to a relationship of retaliation.

The Bible Condemns the Retaliation Relationship Style
The Bible tells us:

> Never pay back evil for evil. Do things in such a way that everyone can see you are honest clear through. Don't quarrel with anyone. Be at peace with everyone, just as much as possible. Dear friends, never avenge yourselves. Leave that to God, for He has said that He will repay those who deserve it. (Don't take the law into your own hands.) Instead, feed your enemy if he is hungry. If he is thirsty give him something to drink and you will be "heaping coals of fire on his head." In other words, he will feel ashamed of himself for what he has done to you. Don't let evil get the upper hand but conquer evil by doing good (Rom. 12:17-21, TLB).

Jesus makes a similar statement in Matthew 5:38-42, and Proverbs 17:9 says, "Love forgets mistakes; nagging about them parts the best of friends" (TLB). And Proverbs 20:22 tells us, "Don't repay evil for evil. Wait for the Lord to handle the matter" (TLB).

Both the Old and New Testaments tell us that retaliation is wrong and should be avoided at all cost. However, retaliation has great appeal to fallen human beings, and too often we find ourselves entangled within the grips of retaliation.

Profile of the Retaliation Relationship Style
We have seen the causes of the retaliation relationship, now let's turn our attention to the actions, activities, and attitudes that fuel this style so strongly rejected by Scripture:

▶ We attempt to make the other person conform to our wishes while neglecting his or her needs.

▶ We begin taking aggressive action toward the other person.

▶ We start viewing the other person as a barrier in the way of getting our needs met.

▶ A struggle for domination and control begins.

▶ The relationship degenerates into perpetual conflict.

▶ Finally someone wins the struggle for domination.

We attempt to make the other person conform to our wishes while neglecting his or her needs. This is usually the first sign that the relationship has changed from cooperation to retaliation. In many instances neither party may be aware of what is happening. However, once we begin focusing on our own needs it doesn't take long for the attempts to become very noticeable.

Following my meeting with Ed and Jaylene that day in the student union, I spent many hours with them listening and understanding why each saw personal needs as more important than those of the other.

One day while we were studying together in the library, Jaylene showed us an article she had cut out of the newspaper. "Ed, did you read this article in this morning's paper?" she said tauntingly. "It sounds like there will be a freeze on all salaries within the Kansas City schools system this fall. If we were to go back there we'd probably both have to get part-time jobs at night just to pay the rent." As she handed Ed the article she gave him a disapproving smile and continued, "Dr.

Edwards, from the business department, says we are fools if we don't take the job in California. What do you think, Myron?"

Jaylene was attempting to make Ed give in to her desires. She was subtly seeking to get Ed to conform to her viewpoint. She was slowly moving their relationship into retaliation.

We begin taking aggressive action toward the other person. When our subtle attempts fail, we begin taking aggressive action and openly try to persuade the other person to do what we want.

For example, as Ed and Jaylene continued to argue over moving to California, she became more and more determined to take the job. She began making fun of Ed, calling him a "mamma's boy," and accusing him of not loving her and of being a male chauvinist. "Why do we always have to do things your way?" she asked Ed as we drank a Coke together. "I've been doing things your way for five years and look where it's gotten me! I think you're just jealous that I can make more than you."

I was embarrassed at the way Jaylene was attacking Ed, and so was he. He tried to laugh at her remarks as if she was only joking, but it was obvious she was serious.

Isn't it amazing we can get so wrapped up in ourselves that we totally overlook how damaging our actions are to others? Once we begin feeding such selfishness we discover it has an insatiable appetite. Once the process begins it is difficult to stop feeding it.

Selfishness is at the root of all relationship problems. It is our self-centeredness that causes us to become so aggressive in our efforts. Once selfishness is allowed out of the cage, the change is immediate. Serving self, instead of others, becomes the priority that negatively transforms our whole attitude toward relationships.

We start viewing the other person as a barrier in the way of getting our needs met. Our commitment to getting our own needs met, at another's expense, causes us to view others in the relationship differently. Once we conclude that the other person is not meeting our needs we begin viewing him or her as the problem. We see them as a barrier in the way of getting what we want.

David saw his mother, Janice, as the obstacle in the way of getting to go live with his father. Therefore, he began lashing out at her. As that failed to work he began threatening to run away in an effort to get around the barrier.

We adults are just as guilty. We also try to overcome barriers—even when they represent the people closest to us—that stand in the way of getting our needs met.

One day I met Jaylene in the hall and when I asked her how things were going she replied, "Things are going awful! Ed and I are fighting all the time about this job I've been offered. He is so jealous. For the first time I'm seeing Ed differently than I've ever seen him before. I am starting to really resent him and all the weaknesses in his personality." She paused for a moment and as if talking to herself said, "Somehow I'm going to make him see I really must take that job. I've just got to make him change his mind."

As we become deeply entrenched in the retaliation relationship style we become more self-centered. It becomes easier to blame others, see their weaknesses, find fault with their actions, and see them as the problem. Viewing others as the problem makes it easier to aggressively attack them with the goal of forcing them to meet our needs.

A struggle for domination and control begins. At this point in the relationship we are seeking to force the other person to agree with us. The battle lines are clearly drawn and the war begins in earnest. And as in the case of most wars, all restraints are thrown off. Anything goes to win the struggle. The forces of selfishness are only as limited as our own creativity.

As the retaliation relationship style degenerates, we begin constant verbal attacks on the individual. We take advantage of every opportunity; we accuse them of being the problem. Their character and emotions are all fair game in the attack. We try to make them look bad in the eyes of others. Finally, we do everything in our power to convince them that they are wrong and we are right.

David accused his mother of not loving him. He tried to make her feel guilty for not letting him live with his father. He defied her authority. However, we must realize that adults are capable of far more serious actions in their struggle for control.

Jaylene began calling Ed's mother and asking her to put pressure on him to move to California. She cut him down in front of the other students in our class. She convinced some of her teachers to encourage Ed to agree to the move. And every time I was around them she brought up the subject, and at one point threatened to go without him if he didn't decide to let her take the job.

The relationship degenerates into perpetual conflict. During relationship seminars I ask the question, "How many of you enjoy being dominated?" and the response is always the same—none. No one likes to be dominated. Therefore, when we discover someone in the relationship is attempting to control us we resist. We fight back. We do everything we can to avoid being controlled.

As a result, the struggle for domination leads to a period of perpetual conflict in the retaliation style relationship. The person we are attempting to control strikes back. Their counterattack includes a point by point retaliation. Our methods of offense become their methods of defense. What started out as covert, subtle actions to get one's needs met turns into a violent, raging war for superiority and control. The devastating outcome is inevitable.

Finally, someone wins the struggle for domination. What appear at first to be minor, innocent acts of selfishness, that give birth to the retaliation style, build and escalate into open and aggressive hostile acts of a full scale conflict. Eventually someone wins the battle for control. We will see later that this victory is only temporary because there are no winners in this type of conflict.

I can still remember, as if it happened yesterday, that day in the coffee shop when Jaylene won the battle and Ed gave in to her demands to move to California. We had just finished eating and as usual they were arguing about her job offer. "You're afraid to move to California because you think you can't get a job anywhere else," Jaylene said. Suddenly her whole countenance changed and she became very serious and rigid. Her voice was cold and hard as she leaned across the table and said, "Ed, I want this job! I want it more than anything I've ever wanted in my life! I suggest you think again before you refuse to go to California. You may be losing more than the additional money I would make there!"

There was dead silence marked by an expressionless pause on Ed's part. I think he knew he had lost even before he said anything. Finally he put his hand over Jaylene's and said, "Okay, Jaylene. I think it is a big mistake, but you win. Call those people and tell them you'll take the job. I don't care. I'll find something to do in California."

Even though neither of them were aware of it at the time, Ed and Jaylene had just entered into a new relationship style. The battle for control was over. There had been a winner and loser. Her needs were being met at his expense. There had been no compromises. Jaylene's self-centeredness had scored a major victory. And as in the case of all "winners," she was elated.

She leaned across the table and with a big smile gave Ed a kiss on the cheek. "I'll make it up to you, Ed," she said. "We'll have a great life in California, you'll see." However, as we will see in the next chapter, the satisfaction of winning the struggle is short-lived.

Traps of the Retaliation Relationship Style
There are numerous traps set along the way to snare those who fall prey to retaliation. And like those of the north woods trapper, they are so well camouflaged that we are ensnared in their jaws unexpectedly and without warning.
▶ The retaliation relationship creates unfulfilled needs.
▶ The retaliation relationship promotes self-centeredness.
▶ The retaliation style creates an atmosphere of conflict within the relationship.

▶ The retaliation style leads to a more damaging relationship.

The retaliation relationship creates unfulfilled needs. Earlier in the chapter we learned that retaliation relationships form because individuals are attempting to get others to meet their needs. However, it is ironic that in the process of trying to do so they only help create additional unfulfilled needs.

Focusing on one's own needs means not concentrating on meeting the needs of others. Therefore, others in the relationship quickly develop unfulfilled needs like your own. So instead of being a relationship type that meets needs, the retaliation style creates additional needs.

The retaliation relationship promotes self-centeredness. Earlier we compared an unfulfilled need to the wayward blow of a hammer to an innocent finger. Our attention is quickly focused in both cases. As we have just observed, when one party in the relationship begins focusing on his or her own needs then the needs of the other person are also left unfulfilled. As a result, a cyclical chain of events begins where the individual is forced to focus on his or her own unfulfilled needs created by the self-centeredness of the other person. And in the cause-and-effect process he or she also is trapped into becoming self-centered.

Just as we can't ignore the physical pain created by the hammer, neither can we ignore the emotional pain created by unfulfilled needs. They do get our attention no matter how hard we try to ignore or spiritualize them. Focusing on one's own needs and ignoring the needs of others sets the cyclical trap in motion and invites others to retaliate in the stifling atmosphere of self-centeredness. It is true that we can, to some degree, control our reactions to our unfulfilled needs, but we can never ignore them—nor should we try.

The retaliation style creates an atmosphere of conflict within the relationship. This creates and promotes negativism. We begin feeling sorry for ourselves because our needs are no longer being met. Criticism and condemnation become the focus of conversation. Our energies are focused on finding fault with those whom we feel are not meeting our needs. The result is a relationship saturated with negativity, hostility, and resentment.

In most cases the issues that caused us to form the retaliation style are replaced by more serious ones and we discover that every issue discussed turns into a major conflict or argument. Before long, conflict becomes an expected and accepted way of life in the relationship.

The retaliation style leads to a more damaging relationship. This is the most deadly of all the traps in the retaliation relationship style. Unless we quickly apply the principles of restoration, we will soon find ourselves moving out of retaliation into domination. And domination style relationships are far more devastating and destructive than retaliation ones.

THE DOMINATION RELATIONSHIP STYLE

5

I was beginning to feel a little uncomfortable as the man sitting across the table silently studied me with a steady gaze, but I made every effort to keep him from detecting my discomfort. He was a lot different than I had pictured him. He was taller and thinner, and his graying hair made him look much older. However, his thin, neatly trimmed black mustache and three-piece, dark-gray, pin-striped suit gave him a very distinguished look.

His name was Charles Stone, and he was sitting in the exact seat Janice had occupied several months earlier as she talked about the hurts she was experiencing since their marriage had fallen apart. I had often wondered what he was like and what his side of the story would be, but I never expected to find out. However, by the time we had finished lunch and six additional cups of coffee, I knew almost as much about Charles and his frustrations as I did about Janice, his former wife.

That is, I knew his perception and interpretation of the problems. It is amazing how two people involved in the same relationship can have such different perceptions of their problems. Charles and Janice were no exception. As I listened to Charles I sometimes wondered if he was talking about the same marriage relationship I had heard his former wife describe.

"I was attracted to Janice because she was a very strong, aggressive woman. She seemed to always know what she wanted and how to get it," he said. "But I didn't know how strong and aggressive she really was until we were married.

65

From the time we started planning our wedding until I finally ran off with Bridgett, Janice made all the final decisions. She always had to have the final say about everything."

Charles' whole personality seemed to change as he talked about Janice. He became almost like a meek child seeking approval, instead of the outgoing, self-secure man I had met earlier in Denver. "We always did everything Janice's way. She totally dominated me. She suffocated my personality. I had to be and do what she wanted," he confessed.

Small beads of perspiration stood out on his forehead as he continued, "I tried to stand up to her but I guess I just wasn't any match for that woman. She could be so sweet and kind in public, but she was like a taskmaster. When she cracked the whip I jumped as high and far as she wanted or there was the devil to pay." He dropped his eyes to the floor and said, "I guess that's what made me finally leave her. Bridgett made me feel like a man again, instead of a mouse in the corner waiting to be trapped."

According to Charles, Janice refused to cut back on her ministry outreach, while they were living in Florida, because she had to prove to him that she could be as productive as he was as a pastor. "She never could stand to be outdone by anyone. She had to be in charge and do better than anyone else."

According to Charles, Janice never wanted to spend time with the kids before they divorced. "The kids were always a bother to her then, but now that I want them, she acts like they are the most important thing in her life," he said with much hurt in his voice. "But I know all she's really doing is making sure both the kids and I know she is still in charge."

As I listened to Charles that day I was reminded of the devastating pain of broken relationships. I remembered my own relationship failures and the difficulty in sorting out fact from opinion under such strenuous circumstances.

Why Domination Relationships Develop
The domination relationship style is born out of the conflicts

that occur in the retaliation mode. In almost all instances relationships move through the retaliation style prior to degenerating into the domination relationship. The retaliation style relationship sets the stage for the more detrimental and damaging domination style. The domination relationship develops for the following reasons:

▶ Winning the struggle for control
▶ Total commitment to self's needs
▶ Development of a superiority attitude

Winning the struggle for control. The retaliation style can be best described as an ongoing struggle for control of the relationship. As we saw in the last chapter, its final stage consists of someone finally winning that struggle for control. At that point we enter the domination relationship style. In fact, we cannot enter into a domination relationship until the struggle for control is over and someone in the relationship emerges as the victor, using that control to get his or her needs met at the expense of others in the relationship.

Initially, the relationship may appear to improve when someone wins the struggle for control and the domination relationship style develops. This frequently occurs when there is a rapid decrease in open, hostile conflict. The war appears to be over. The battles subside and what appears to be a "cease-fire" occurs.

As the domination relationship emerges there is usually a lull in the fighting because both sides have tired of the constant state of siege that prevailed during the latter stages of the retaliation stage. There is a temporary effort on both sides to avoid further conflict. This is especially true of the person who just lost the struggle. He or she is not only exhausted from the conflict, but still suffering from the sting of defeat. Unfortunately, this plays right into the hand of the now dominant party in the relationship. It makes it easier for the person winning control to take charge of the relationship and use his or her new-found power as victor to establish dominancy in the relationship.

Total commitment to self's needs. The domination relationship style is marked by a total commitment to self's needs. The struggle for control of the relationship began because an individual was committed to getting his or her needs met. Once a person wins that struggle, the commitment to get one's needs met at the expense of others becomes even stronger.

The person winning the struggle for control is responsible for the relationship moving from retaliation to domination. That shift in relationship styles is not only the result of winning the struggle for control, but is also due to the "winner's" total commitment to self's needs. The commitment to getting others to serve self's needs becomes stronger. As a result, the control of others in the relationship becomes greater. The longer a relationship remains in a domination style the greater the dominator's control over the relationship.

Development of a superiority attitude. As you will recall from the last chapter, people winning the struggle for control usually feel that their needs are more important than those of others in the relationship. Therefore, they feel a right to have their needs met at the expense of others.

If we feel our needs are more important than those of others, we soon conclude we are more important than other people. We begin developing an attitude of superiority. If confronted, we probably would deny such an attitude, but our actions speak far louder than our words.

The dominator won the struggle for control with the attitude that self needs are more important than those of others. Therefore, the dominator isn't going to change the attitude that helped gain control of the relationship in the first place. Instead of changing that attitude of superiority, the dominator will become more convinced of the inalienable right to have needs fulfilled at another person's expense. The stronger that attitude becomes the more committed the dominator will be to maintaining that relationship style once it develops.

Domination Relationships from God's Viewpoint
Ecclesiastes 4:1-3 gives a very accurate description of the domination relationship style and its results:

Again I looked and saw all the oppression that was taking place under the sun: I saw the tears of the oppressed—and they have no comforter; power was on the side of their oppressors—and they have no comforter. And I declared that the dead, who had already died, are happier than the living, who are still alive. But better than both is he who has not yet been, who has not seen the evil that is done under the sun.

Let's look at this passage point by point. The writer begins by saying, "Again I looked and saw all the oppression that was taking place under the sun." This applies to people in domination relationships because the dominator certainly is oppressing those under his or her control.

Next the writer describes what the oppressed are experiencing. "I saw the tears of the oppressed—and they have no comforter." This is an excellent description of what occurs in a domination relationship style. Those being dominated are filled with hurts and emotional pain; however, they get no comfort from the dominator. The person controlling them is so caught up in a power trip that he or she is usually not aware of the emotional pain being inflicted.

Notice what the last part of verse 1 says, "Power was on the side of their oppressors—and they have no comforter." Dominators have all the power in a domination style relationship. They are in complete charge. However, as the verse points out, they also are not really fulfilled in the relationship. They too need a comforter, but do not have one. This is a classic description of what occurs to both the oppressor and oppressed in a domination relationship.

Verse 2 gives us clear insight as to just how terrible a domination relationship is: "And I declared that the dead, who had already died, are happier than the living, who are still alive." This passage points out that people who have to exist under such oppression eventually conclude they would be better off dead than continue to suffer under the abuse of domination. That is very strong language. However, I have had many people, suffering at the hands of a dominator, express those exact same feelings to me.

Verse 3 uses even stronger language to condemn the domination relationship style: "But better than both is he who has not yet been, who has not seen the evil that is done under the sun." It is better to have never been born than to have to experience the terrible pain of oppression in a domination relationship.

This is a sobering passage that pictures God's contempt for domination relationship styles. It clearly points out the failure of both the oppressor and the oppressed to support and comfort one another from the hurts and pains they are experiencing. These verses warn of the tragedy of domination style relationships and should motivate us to avoid their snare.

Characteristics of a Domination Relationship Style

To get a clearer understanding of this relationship style, we must learn its specific characteristics. The traits of the domination relationship style are as follows:

▶ The person being dominated begins to avoid conflict.
▶ The personality of the individual being dominated is suffocated.
▶ The dominated person's creativity is stifled.
▶ The oppressed person eventually becomes the slave of the dominator.
▶ The person under domination resorts to manipulation.
▶ Both parties lose respect for the other.
▶ The dominated person eventually moves to an "isolation" style.

The person being dominated begins to avoid conflict. This happens during the early stages of the domination relationship. It allows the person in control of the relationship to establish dominancy and to take charge of the decision-making process.

Whether it is done readily or reluctantly matters not. The dominated person tends to give in to the dominator in an effort to avoid conflict and resistance that will only worsen the relationship. As a result, over a period of time the dominated passively assume a course of least resistance, giving in to the demands of the dominator. In this way, once the initial struggle for power is over, the dominator usually is able to control the relationship and those in it with little, if any, additional hindrance.

Those being dominated soon learn to accept their submissive role, passively suffering in silence. Although their needs are continually neglected, they continue methodically serving the needs of the dominator. During the early stages of this relationship style the person being oppressed continues to believe that the dominator will once again voluntarily start meeting the needs of the dominated. However, in most cases this is false hope.

Once the dominator begins using others to get his needs met he is very reluctant to voluntarily change. That does not mean there isn't hope for the relationship to improve. But that usually does not occur until the dominator is confronted with the fact that his continued oppressive actions may lead to the destruction of the relationship.

Unfortunately, during the early stages of the domination style most people aren't willing to confront the dominator with the possibility that the relationship may be doomed to failure. As long as those being dominated remain fearful of confrontation the dominator will more than likely continue to exercise control at their expense.

The personality of the individual being dominated is suffocated. Generally, as the dominated person gives in to the dominator the relationship worsens until eventually the personality of the oppressed one is suffocated. The dominated person will be required to mimic the actions and follow the dictates of the dominator. As the grip of control grows the oppressed person loses the freedom of individuality. No longer free to express personal opinions, the dominated one's fate is to blindly follow the whims of the dominator. Like Charles Stone, the dominated feel that they must jump when the dominator cracks the whip.

Once Jaylene Parker won the struggle for control she began to suffocate her husband's personality. I watched as Jaylene took charge of the entire relationship. She not only took the job, but left Ed with his mother while she flew to California to find them a place to live.

Upon returning she announced that they would have to take money out of savings to buy a new wardrobe for both herself and Ed since he would be attending corporate social functions with her. She proceeded to outfit him with new clothes the way a mother would a small child, making all the decisions, even down to the color of the new ties she wanted him to wear.

Ed made a few feeble attempts to inject his opinions, but Jaylene assured him that she knew the latest West Coast styles and he would just have to trust her judgment. Jaylene was rapidly tightening her grip as Ed became nothing more than a passive player in the relationship.

The dominated person's creativity is stifled. Those being controlled by the dominator rarely, if ever, have the opportunity to make important decisions. The decisions they do get to make usually must have the approval of the dominator, or they are vetoed.

During my conversation with Charles Stone he said, "We always had to do everything Janice's way. Oh, she was good at making it look like it was my idea, but if she didn't approve, things just didn't happen." Charles' observation is a classic description of the domination style. The dominator maintains control over the relationship by controlling the decisions within it. And such control greatly stifles the creativity of those being dominated.

The dominator's failure to use the input of those being dominated is one of the great tragedies of the domination relationship style. It too quickly destroys what little self-image those being oppressed may still have. It creates strong resentments toward the dominator and greatly reduces the potential productivity of the relationship.

The oppressed person eventually becomes the slave of the

dominator. The dominator has no more regard for the needs of those he is dominating than a master has for the desires of a slave. Charles described Janice as a "taskmaster." That is a good description of the oppressor in a domination relationship style. The oppressor uses people for selfish gain, and when they are all used up, doesn't hesitate to find another warm body to take their place.

That is why the dominator in a marriage relationship tends to overpower other family members as well. If she can't get what she wants out of one family member, she will get it out of another. She uses the entire family for only one purpose—to get her needs met at their expense.

The person under domination resorts to manipulation. People being dominated in a relationship inevitably build up an enormous amount of frustration because their needs are no longer being met. The desire to have their own needs fulfilled causes these individuals to resort to manipulation. However, it should be pointed out that attempts to manipulate the dominator are never successful. That is, manipulation never brings about the desired results of permanently changing the dominator. In fact, in almost all instances attempts at manipulation backfire and cause the relationship to deteriorate further.

Ed and Jaylene had joint bank accounts. Shortly following the buying spree that replaced both of their wardrobes, Ed closed out their accounts and put all of the money into an account in his name only. I was at Ed's apartment that afternoon studying for our final exams. He said, "I'm sure Jaylene will be mad when she finds out, but I had to do something to try and regain some voice in the decisions being made around here."

The next day I saw Ed after one of our classes and he said, "Myron, you left just in time yesterday. When Jaylene found out what I had done we had a terrible fight and I had to go put the money back in joint accounts this morning. She was threatening to leave me if I didn't." He shook his head in dejection and said, "She'll probably leave me anyway someday. When she gets in her new job she'll probably find some rising, young executive and pitch me in the trash can."

I couldn't believe the change that had come over Ed. When we entered graduate school together he was an excited, enthusiastic young man. Now he seemed like a lost, dejected puppy. His futile attempt to manipulate his way back into the decision-making process only seemed to discourage him all the more.

The dominated person eventually moves to "isolation." Once the dominated person resorts to manipulation and discovers that it doesn't solve the problems he quickly moves to a new relationship style I call "isolation." In the next chapter we will take a close look at this style and the end result of its very destructive method of dealing with people. However, let's first look at the various false assumptions of the domination style relationship.

False Assumptions

People operating in a domination relationship tend to develop false assumptions about themselves and others within the relationship. The most common ones are listed below:

▶ Dominated people frequently believe they deserve to be treated badly.

▶ The person under domination doesn't acknowledge what is happening and tends to make excuses for the dominator's actions.

▶ The dominator is convinced that the other person or people in the relationship do not have unfulfilled needs.

▶ The dominator believes she knows what is best for the other(s) in the relationship.

Dominated people frequently believe they deserve to be treated badly. There are many reasons why people develop such attitudes, but the biggest is the poor self-image that develops from oppression over an extended period of time. People oppressed in a domination relationship begin to develop negative attitudes about themselves.

During a relationship seminar one lady who obviously had been dominated by her husband for many years said, "I feel so guilty when I let myself think about my own needs. I guess I've convinced myself I don't really have a right to have my needs met." Unfortunately there are numerous people in such relationships who have arrived at the same false assumptions. They not only feel guilty for thinking about their own needs, they actually don't believe they deserve to have those needs met.

If you are such a person I want to assure you that you deserve to have your needs fulfilled and you don't deserve to be oppressed in a relationship. You must be willing to make your needs known again and make it clear that a domination relationship is not acceptable. In a later chapter we will discuss in detail the process of turning a domination type back into a cooperation style.

The person under domination doesn't acknowledge what is happening and tends to make excuses for the dominator's actions. This frequently occurs because the person being dominated assumes that if she ignores reality the problem will go away. Therefore, she makes excuses for the dominator's actions and may even blame herself for the way she is being treated.

However, the problem won't go away by itself. And instead of making excuses, the person being dominated must be willing to confront the dominator with his actions. As long as you make excuses for the dominator he will continue his oppressive activity.

The dominator is convinced that the other person or people in the relationship do not have unfulfilled needs. The dominator gets so caught up in self that he not only forgets about the needs of others, but convinces himself they don't have unfulfilled needs. The dominator frequently assumes that if his need is being met everyone's needs are being met also.

The dominator believes she knows what is best for the other(s) in the relationship. Almost all dominators believe they know what is best for those they are dominating. And they also believe they are best qualified to make the decisions for everyone in the relationship.

This is one of the reasons the dominator tends to resist input from others in the relationship. She is often more willing to take advice from those outside the relationship than from within because she feels superior to those she is dominating.

The dominator always assumes she is right and others in the relationship are wrong if they challenge her. As a result, many dominators actually feel they need to be in charge in order to protect and care for others in the relationship. This may be true in some instances when dealing with small children, but it certainly isn't justifiable when dealing with adults.

Spiritualizing Domination Relationships

Many Christians wind up in domination relationship styles because of their spiritual convictions. In some religious circles there is an overemphasis on the husband as leader in the home and church with the wife in a submissive role.

I believe that the husband needs to be the leader in the home; however, I strongly disagree with the way some husbands carry out their leadership role. In my book, *The New Leader,* I tell of a couple that represents a classic example of this type of relationship.

While I was conducting a management seminar in Kansas City Mr. and Mrs. Jones invited me to attend church and have lunch with them prior to catching a plane Sunday afternoon. The Joneses picked me up at my hotel and as I started to get in the backseat of their car with their son, Mr. Jones said, "No, no, Myron, you sit up here in the front seat with me, my wife can get in the backseat with Johnny."

I explained that I would rather sit in the back and let them sit together in the front, but Mr. Jones insisted that his wife get in the back and I sit in the front with him.

On the way to the church he assured me I would enjoy the service. He said that their pastor was delivering a series of messages on the home. All the way to the church he talked about the importance of the husband assuming his biblical role as head over the home and family.

By the time we got to the church I was furious with the way Mr. Jones had been treating his wife. During our ride to the church Mr. Jones picked on his wife. Every time she made a statement, he either disagreed or tried to correct her. After church he scolded her for spending so much time talking to friends. When we got to their home, he criticized her for leaving the Sunday paper scattered on the floor. He even criticized the great meal she had fixed. While picking on his wife, he punctuated his criticism of her by expressing concern that more husbands should learn to apply biblical principles of leadership in their homes.

While waiting to catch a plane that afternoon I felt sorry for both Mr. and Mrs. Jones. I hurt for her because she had to put up with his insensitivity, and I felt sorry for him because he thought he had to intimidate his wife in order to be a leader. He obviously was in charge of his family, but he certainly wasn't displaying the kind of love for his wife that the Bible commands. His major concern was to make sure his family was submissive to his instructions.

I think of the Jones family often and wonder how long their marriage can last. Their relationship certainly wasn't based on biblical principles, even though he spent the entire day extolling their superiority.

If we want to follow scriptural principles of leadership for the home we should study Matthew 20:25-28 which says, "You know that the rulers of the Gentiles lord it over them, and their high officials exercise authority over them. Not so with you. Instead, whoever wants to become great among you must be your servant, and whoever wants to be first must be your slave—just as the Son of Man did not come to be served, but to serve, and to give His life as a ransom for many."

According to this passage a leader is a servant. And a servant meets the needs of those he serves. One can't follow biblical principles of leadership and maintain a domination relationship style. The kind of leader God intends must apply the passage just quoted as well as Philippians 2:3-4: "Do nothing out of selfish ambition or vain conceit, but in humility consider others better than yourselves. Each of you should look not only to your own interests, but also to the interests of others." Failure to apply these principles will lead to a domination relationship that violates God's direct command.

THE ISOLATION RELATIONSHIP STYLE

6

Before his company transferred him to Texas, Henry Burmeister and I used to do a lot of fishing together. Henry was normally a very jolly fellow and a good fishing buddy. However, on one particular fishing trip he was extremely quiet and his thoughts seemed to be a million miles away.

Several times during the day I asked him if he felt okay and each time he gave a faint smile and assured me he was fine. However, on the way home he finally began talking and I soon learned the truth. "Myron, what would you do if your wife stopped talking to you?" Henry asked as he munched on the last of the cookies I had brought for our lunch.

Before I could answer he continued, "My wife and I are having big problems. I know something has been bothering her for a long time, but she refuses to talk about it. In fact, most of the time she treats me like I'm not even in the same room with her." Henry took off his fishing hat, scratched his thick mop of silver white hair, looked at me and said, "Do you think it would do any good if you talked to her? Do you think maybe she'd tell you what's wrong? I sure can't solve a problem if I don't know what it is."

A few days later I made a point to drop by Henry's house before he got home from work and told Maggie, his wife, I needed to see him about repairing one of my fishing rods. She offered me a piece of angel food cake and hot tea and before long Maggie was telling me her story.

She and Henry had been married 32 years. They had three children and seven grandchildren. According to Maggie, she and Henry got along just fine as long as the kids were young and living at home, but when they grew up and left their marriage seemed to "sort of dry up and die on the vine." They never had any big fights, but Maggie felt Henry didn't listen to her or respect her feelings or opinions.

"He always thought he was right and I was wrong," she said as she cut me another piece of her delicious cake. "We never really yelled at each other, but over the years we both learned how to get in our little jabs at the right time." As she poured me another cup of herb tea she shrugged her shoulders and said, "We just slowly drifted apart and now I have nothing more to say. Henry wouldn't listen to me anyway, so it's better this way. At least we aren't yelling at each other. I figure it's a good way to keep from being criticized, and as long as I keep my mouth shut, it helps keep the peace. And the good Lord knows we're both too old to get a divorce now."

She made a feeble attempt to laugh as if it were a big joke, but I could tell by her countenance that her pain was about to bring her to tears.

Then the door opened and as Henry walked in Maggie gathered her composure, poured a fresh cup of hot herb tea for him, and disappeared down the hall. I drank another cup of tea, gave Henry my fishing rod to be repaired, and drove home realizing that Maggie Burmeister was in an isolation relationship style with her husband, Henry.

The Cause of Isolation Relationships

The dominated person takes the first step into the isolation style. At some point in the domination relationship the oppressed person realizes that some changes must take place in order to continue existing in the current relationship. As a result, he or she initiates the isolation relationship style in an attempt to cope with the dominator and the painful situations within the relationship.

The person being oppressed by the dominator slowly becomes more depressed and frustrated with the relationship. Realizing the relationship is getting worse, the oppressed one doesn't see much possibility of it improving. That conclusion causes the dominated person to attempt to manipulate the dominator back into a cooperation relationship style. However, those attempts usually fail and instead of the relationship improving it gets worse.

At that point the person under domination gives up and develops the following feelings that lead to the isolation relationship style:

▶ The dominated person develops a feeling of rejection.
▶ The dominated person develops a feeling of hopelessness.
▶ The dominated person develops feelings of bitterness and resentment.

These feelings develop and continue to build during the domination relationship style and are the main cause of the dominated person moving into the isolation relationship.

The dominated person develops a feeling of rejection. Remember Maggie's description of her relationship with Henry: "We just slowly drifted apart and now I have nothing more to say." As I listened to Maggie that day I could hear the pain of rejection in her voice and see it on her face. The strong feelings of rejection are the result of the dominator's total neglect for the needs of the other.

The person being oppressed ultimately concludes he isn't loved, appreciated, or needed. In most cases he decides he is not capable of making a meaningful contribution to the relationship. These feelings cause the dominated person to withdraw to protect his battered emotions from more pain of rejection.

Most of us do not handle rejection very well. In fact, we usually attempt to avoid it at all costs. During relationship seminars I ask the audience, "How many of you get up each morning with the goal of seeing how many times you can be rejected that day?" No hands are ever raised. The human goal is to be accepted in our relationships.

Each of us has a deep need for acceptance. That is one of the major reasons for forming relationships. Thus the reason for devastation in discovering rejection. The stronger the emotional ties in the relationship, the greater the emotional hurts when one is rejected.

Unfortunately, even when confronted, most people dominating a relationship refuse to admit they are rejecting those they are dominating. For example, Jaylene Parker didn't think she was dominating Ed when she insisted on making his clothing decisions. Janice Stone didn't think she was dominating Charles, even though she had to make or approve all family decisions. Jaylene and Janice didn't believe they were rejecting their mates; they thought they were doing those things for their mates. They saw themselves as "serving" those they loved.

I certainly didn't think I was rejecting my wife. I thought just the opposite. I believed I was a good provider and doing lots of things for my wife. However, I was doing things that met my need, not things that she wanted to do. I bought her the car I wanted her to have. We dined at the places I wanted to eat. I bought the things I wanted her to have. My time with her was spent doing the things I wanted to do.

However, I along with Janice and Jaylene were neglecting the needs of our mates. We weren't considering our mates in our decisions. As a result, the things we did for our mates drove them further from us because we rejected their basic need to be involved in the decision-making process. Such feelings of rejection inevitably cause the person being dominated to move to isolation.

The dominated person develops a feeling of hopelessness. Once the dominated person attempts to manipulate her way back to cooperation and discovers she has not only failed, but made the relationship worse, she develops feelings of hopelessness. She concludes the relationship is not going to improve and her needs are not going to be met. She realizes her failure to correct the situation and finally decides to stop trying. Aware that she is wasting the effort, she resigns herself to learning to live with the situation. At that point she begins moving into an isolation relationship with the dominator.

It is difficult to cope with feelings of hopelessness. Most

suicides are committed by people who develop feelings of hopelessness and are no longer able to cope with the situation. People in isolation relationships also feel an inability to cope with such situations. They conclude the dominator will never change, never accept their views, and never meet their needs. Therefore, to continue in the relationship, they move into isolation.

The isolation style is their way of trying to escape further emotional pain. It allows them the opportunity to retreat and lick their wounds in the privacy of their own inner world. However, it does not solve the problem, but only compounds it.

The dominated person develops feelings of bitterness and resentment. People in isolation relationships have one thing in common—pent-up anger and hostility toward the dominator. These feelings of bitterness, resentment, and hostility are fueled by the rejection and hopelessness already present.

The feelings that lead to an isolation relationship style are extremely negative. As a result, the people who move into isolation are usually disagreeable individuals. They are unable to see anything positive in the relationship and usually dwell on the negative concerning themselves. As we will see, these problems become greater the further one goes into the isolation style. Eventually the relationship falls apart, destroyed from the inside out. In the end, each individual in the relationship plays an important role in its destruction.

Isolation Violates Biblical Principles

The Bible makes it clear that God does not condone isolation relationships. Many people feel justified in developing and maintaining such relationships because of the way they have been treated in domination styles. However, isolation is only an advanced, more severe form of retaliation. It is not only a way of coping but a way of revenge to "get even" with the dominator. However, like manipulation, it is never successful in restoring the relationship to cooperation. Isolation often leads to termination rather than restoration.

That is why the Bible so strongly condemns such actions. The Romans 12:17-21 passage that we looked at earlier certainly applies to the isolation relationship as well. And notice what Galatians 5:15 tells us, "If you keep on biting and devouring each other, watch out or you will be destroyed by each other." The Romans passage warns against repaying evil with evil. The verse in Galatians tells us that if we do, the relationship will be destroyed.

The Isolation Relationship Style in Action
The isolation relationship style is marked by a lack of communication and frequent displays of emotional frustration. During the isolation relationship, the following activities and situations exist:

▶ The other person is mentally blocked out.
▶ Communication is almost nonexistent.
▶ Mistrust of others in the relationship skyrockets.
▶ More problems develop and remain unsolved.
▶ More needs develop and remain unfulfilled.
▶ Each individual becomes more self-centered.
▶ Emotional problems continually increase.
▶ A total lack of concern for the other's needs.
▶ Eventually the relationship will end unless the restoration process beings.

The other person is mentally blocked out. Here the dominated person begins mentally blocking out the dominator in an attempt to avoid further emotional trauma.

The day Henry talked to me about his problems revealed an obvious example of mental blocking on Maggie's part—"I know something has been bothering her for a long time, but she refuses to talk about it. In fact, most of the time she treats me like I'm not even in the same room with her."

That is common practice of people in isolation. They are able to completely ignore others by acting as if they don't exist. The other person is not only mentally blocked out, but usually physically avoided as well. Such action is a common occurrence when an individual is operating in an isolation relationship style.

When Ed Parker began operating in an isolation relationship with Jaylene he found a multitude of things to occupy his time and energies to avoid dealing with her. Jaylene told me, "When Ed is around the house with free time all he does is read, listen to the stereo with his headset on, or talk on the phone to his friends. He never talks to me, even when I talk to him."

That is a typical scenario in an isolation relationship style. The oppressed avoids the dominator by mentally blocking him out. This is one of the ways they try to deal with their emotional pain.

Communication is almost nonexistent. People in isolation relationships can go for days, even weeks, without effectively communicating. They carry on the minimum amount of conversation required to maintain order in the relationship, but they refuse to discuss the real issues.

Communication is to a relationship what blood is to the human body. If the blood supply is cut off from the hand, numbness quickly develops and the person loses the use of that hand. And if the blood remains cut off from the hand, eventually the flesh withers and the hand develops gangrene. If the gangrene is left unattended, it will spread to the rest of the body and bring death to the person. In like manner, if communication is cut off in a relationship for an extended period, the relationship will eventually be destroyed.

When the person in isolation starts mentally blocking out the other person, refusing to communicate, she may be contributing to the problems in the relationship and in fact, be hastening its total destruction. The irony is that she moved into isolation as a means of coping with the problems generated by the dominator, and winds up helping to create just as many problems herself because of her refusal to communicate.

Mistrust of others in the relationship skyrockets. Once communication breaks down, mistrust invades the relationship. The person in isolation becomes suspicious of the dominator's actions and motives, always thinking the worst possible thing. Over a period of time as communication remains stifled, the dominator also begins mistrusting the actions of the person in isolation because neither one really knows what the other is thinking or feeling and a mutual mistrust evolves.

The parties become trapped by their own thoughts, fears, and suspicions. Communication breaks down, and they frequently become paranoid, misinterpreting every word and action.

For example, during my conversation with Charles Stone he admitted that for the last couple of years he and Janice were married communication was almost nonexistent between them. "It got so bad we started passing information back and forth to each other through our kids. Janice would tell David to tell me something and I'd tell him to give her my answer. And to make matters worse, we rarely saw each other," he said.

He explained that during that time they both developed a strong mistrust of each other. "We accused each other of trying to turn the kids against us. We blamed each other for spending money secretly when the checkbook wouldn't balance. Each of us accused the other of using competition in the ministry." His eyes dropped from mine and he continued. "And we both thought the other one was seeing another person."

Charles said Janice began accusing him of infidelity and he thought she was involved with a guy at the radio station. "Every time the phone rang she would eavesdrop if the call was for me," he said in disgust. "If I was gone too long to the store she thought I was meeting some woman. I accused her of spending too much time at the radio station because I thought she liked the general manager."

Charles explained that he had never been interested in other women all the years they had been married until he met Bridgett. "I wanted our marriage to work. I wanted to help other people and be the kind of Christian example they could follow," he said. "But the more mistrust grew between us the less I began to care about us. I guess I finally just gave up, and when I started counseling with Sam and Bridgett I discovered she was having the same problem with Sam that I was having with Janice." He shrugged his broad shoulders and continued. "At first that sort of drew us together, and I guess you know the rest."

Charles and Janice are a classic example of what can happen in an isolation relationship once communication breaks down and mistrust evolves. Even though the relationship may not end the way the Stones' did, the mistrust will slowly destroy anything that may have been left to salvage. Even if the people can stay together physically, emotionally they will be divorced. Mistrust is to a relationship what terminal cancer is to the body—both eventually kill their victim.

More problems develop and remain unsolved. At this point in the relationship the individuals are rapidly moving further and further apart. Each individual in the relationship has begun building barriers to be protected from the deadly missiles of mistrust that are being fired by the other person in the relationship.

An outward silence and inward mistrust evolve to help create a mountain of unsolved problems within the relationship. As the individuals retreat behind their walls of defense they discover that instead of providing protection, the walls only create more serious unsolved problems.

More needs develop and remain unfulfilled. The silence and mistrust lead to communication problems that help create more personal needs. In fact, the fragile relationship seems destined to be torn to pieces by the violent rage at the eye of a storm of unfulfilled needs.

At this point in the relationship neither the dominator nor the person being dominated is having needs met. What had once been a beautiful, productive relationship is now nothing more than isolated individuals coexisting in a lonely battle zone.

Each person becomes more self-centered. Earlier we examined how an unfulfilled need gets our attention. Therefore in the isolation relationship as more needs emerge each individual becomes more self-centered. Instead of being able to focus on meeting the needs of the other, each person's attention is directed toward the hurt and pain of unfulfilled needs.

Self becomes the main center of attraction in an isolation relationship style. Individuals tend to gravitate between self-pity and hostile resentment toward the other person in the relationship.

Emotional problems continually increase. As individuals focus on themselves, the more aware they become of their emotional pain and the more they resent those who have failed to meet their needs.

A total lack of concern for the other person's needs. Eventually the isolation relationship breaks down to the point where those involved have no concern for the needs of others. They not only fail to meet others' needs in the relationship, but they make a conscious decision to neglect those needs.

Eventually the relationship will end unless the restoration process begins. The isolation style is the last stop on the journey prior to terminating the relationship. Couples entering divorce court are in isolation. The have lived and died through the stages of mental-blocking, communication breakdown, unsolved problems, and unfulfilled needs. Finally, they have reached a point of insensitivity to the other person's needs.

However, often in Christian marriages the relationship terminates emotionally but the couple keep up a front by continuing to live together. They fail to divorce and physically part ways, but their emotional separation is just as complete as those who do. This type of situation is as destructive and unbiblical as actually terminating the relationship through legal means.

Earlier I mentioned my aunt and uncle who lived together for years in an isolation relationship. They occupied the same house and remained legally married, but they were mentally and emotionally separated. They not only made one another miserable, but everyone with whom they had intimate contact. They were the subject of many private jokes within our family and the community where they lived. Sadly, they went to their graves having failed to reconcile their differences.

Happy Beginnings with Unhappy Endings
Figure 5 below compares the cooperation and relationship styles. As the comparison illustrates, the cooperation relationship begins on a positive and fulfilling note. However, by the time the relationship deteriorates into isolation, things have changed drastically. Instead of the relationship being a source of mutual satisfaction, it has become a source of mutual irritation.

THE COOPERATION STYLE	THE ISOLATION STYLE
*A strong commitment to meet the other person's needs. *Strong mutual trust and respect. *Joint decision-making and problem-solving. *Willingness to be transparent. *Willingness to forgive and forget mistakes. *Strong emphasis on teamwork. *The relationship grows stronger.	*Others are mentally blocked out. *Communication stops. *Mistrust skyrockets. *Problems remain unsolved. *Needs remain unfulfilled. *Emotional pain and hostility continue to increase. *A lack of concern for others' needs exists. *The relationship will probably end.

FIGURE 5: This diagram compares the cooperation and isolation relationship styles.

By comparing the beginning and ending of the relationship we can clearly see the devastating effect of selfishness. During the cooperation relationship the emphasis is on meeting the needs of others. There is a deemphasis on self. However, as one moves away from cooperation there is a greater emphasis on getting self needs met at the expense of others. Self becomes lord over the relationship.

The more emphasis we place on self in a relationship the more unfulfilling that relationship becomes. On the other hand, the more those in the relationship emphasize meeting the needs of each other, the more rewarding that relationship will be.

The Breaking Point

Most people in isolation relationship styles eventually reach "the breaking point." That is, they conclude the relationship is no longer worth the effort they are investing. They are tired of the rejection. They feel hopeless in their efforts and no longer have the physical and emotional strength to continue fighting. At that point they are ready to terminate the relationship.

That happened to me and my wife while we were living in Alaska. We went through the isolation relationship style and finally I gave up and said, "I quit. I want a divorce." Even though we didn't actually get a divorce until several years later, I can tell you that divorce is usually not the solution. In fact, in most instances it is the beginning of even greater problems.

I realize there are rare instances when this is not the case and a divorce or termination of a relationship may be needed—whether this be a work relationship, friendship, or family contact. However, as a general rule, *people within relationships need to change instead of changing relationships.* In the next chapter we will discuss the step-by-step process one must go through to return a relationship to cooperation.

THE ROAD TO RESTORATION

7

When Henry Burmeister called to let me know he had fixed my fishing rod, I jokingly told him to tell Maggie to have another piece of her delicious angel food cake ready for me when I came by the next afternoon. I deliberately got there about an hour before Henry got home from work to talk to Maggie again about their relationship. And before long Maggie was once again talking about her problems with Henry.

When I asked how long they were going to let the problems continue she replied, "We've tried to solve our problems for years, but things just keep getting worse. I guess we don't know anything else to do to make it better, so we just try to stay out of each other's way." As I listened to Maggie that afternoon I was again reminded of the demise of my own marriage. I was very eager for hers to be restored while there was still time.

Why Restoration Is Difficult

The further away a relationship moves from cooperation the more difficult it is to restore it to that ideal style. It is much easier to return to cooperation from retaliation than it is from domination or from the extreme of isolation. That is why it is important to begin the restoration process at the first signs of decay in the relationship. If you wait until the relationship has deteriorated too far the possibility of restoring it to cooperation is remote.

There are many reasons why restoration is difficult, for every relational situation is unique. But there are major factors

that commonly block the restoration process.
▶ Unwillingess to believe the other person will change.
▶ Unwillingness to forgive.
▶ Fear to risk being hurt again.
▶ Desire for revenge.
▶ Our pride interferes.
▶ Inability to forget the past.

Unwillingness to believe the other person will change. One evening I had an opportunity to discuss Henry and Maggie's relationship problems with them. They both admitted they didn't believe the other was willing to change. During our conversation Henry said, "How can you have a good relationship with a wife who gives you the silent treatment every time she gets upset?" He began raising his voice as he continued, "I'm not a mind reader! I can't solve a problem if I don't know what it is!" He shook his head, looked at Maggie, and said, "I'm tired of playing guessing games with you. But I figured out a long time ago that you aren't about to change. That's just the way you are, so I try to live with it."

Maggie set her cup of tea down hard spilling it on the table-top and yelled, "I'm tired of you always blaming me for our problems. You're the one who always has to do it your way. You're the one who won't listen. You never have, and you never will!"

It soon became apparent that both of them thought the other was to blame and neither believed the other was willing to change. Both of them had concluded it was impossible to improve their relationship so they weren't trying. This is a typical attitude in isolation relationships. They have decided the situation is hopeless. Such attitudes make it difficult to start down the road to restoration.

Unwillingness to forgive. This is another major roadblock in the restoration process. There can be no restoration without forgiveness. However, it is difficult to forgive people for an offense you are convinced they are going to commit against you again.

When I suggested to Henry and Maggie that they forgive

each other for the past, Maggie quickly replied, "Huh! It's pretty hard to forgive someone when you know they are going to just continue hurting you. I forgave Henry in the past, but it didn't change the way he treated me. He's going to have to show me he is sincere before I forgive him again."

However, our forgiveness can't be conditional if we want to restore the relationship to cooperation. I will admit it is hard to continue forgiving someone when you feel they aren't going to repent. But I can assure you from observing the lives of many others, that the relationship can never be restored to cooperation as long as you fail to forgive the other person. Forgiveness must be unconditional.

Fear to risk being hurt again. There is always risk involved in attempting to restore a relationship to cooperation and one of the greatest risks taken is the possibility of being hurt again. However, like the willingness to forgive, the restoration process cannot occur until one is willing to risk being hurt again.

Unfortunately, by the time a relationship reaches the latter stages of domination or isolation people have been hurt so many times that it is difficult for them to forgive and start rebuilding the relationship. As a result, the fear of being hurt keeps many people from taking the risks required to reestablish cooperation.

People erect barriers as a means of protection against the emotional pain caused by the others in the relationship. Therefore, it is difficult for some folks to stop hiding behind those walls and come into the open and run the risk of further abuse. But such risks are essential to rebuilding a cooperation relationship.

Desire for revenge. As long as one is seeking revenge there is no hope for reestablishing a cooperation relationship. Attempts to get even have caused many relationships to degenerate until they were totally destroyed.

During the evening with Henry and Maggie he admitted, "Every time Maggie goes on one of her silence campaigns I get so angry I pay her back by doing things to irritate her." And

Maggie retorted, "Yes, I know you do. And that just makes me more determined to avoid you because I know it upsets you!"

We must realize there is no such thing as "getting even" in a deteriorating relationship. Such attempts only lead to stronger retaliatory measures on the part of all concerned. It becomes a vicious circle of "one-upmanship." Instead of getting even one is actually destroying the relationship. Restoration can never begin until all involved stop seeking revenge.

Our pride interferes. Pride is probably the biggest stumbling block in the way of restoring our relationships to a cooperation style. Pride frequently hinders us from thinking logically, acting rationally, and reacting properly. The attitudes of pride make it difficult for us to ask for forgiveness, stop seeking revenge, admit we were wrong, and commit to putting the needs of others first. All of these must occur if we expect to restore the relationship to cooperation.

As people begin rebuilding a cooperation relationship they discover that pride, more than any other single factor, hinders them. It causes them to conclude that they are right and others are wrong. It encourages people to get even. It stimulates them to expect others to ask for forgiveness instead of them. Pride tells them they would be showing signs of weakness if they asked for forgiveness.

As long as we let pride control us we will never be able to reestablish a cooperation relationship style. We need to realize that it was pride that helped damage the relationship in the first place. Therefore, if we persist in promoting pride we can be assured that the relationship will continue to deteriorate instead of develop.

Inability to forget the past. To rebuild a strong relationship for the future we must be willing to let go of the past. Bringing up the past and dwelling on previous shortcomings greatly hinders the restoration process. It isn't enough to verbalize forgiveness; a conscious decision to stop dwelling on past offenses must be made. We will never totally forget the trespasses, but they certainly need not haunt our thoughts nor dominate our conversations.

Focusing on the past pains only serves to remind you of where you've been and insures your quick return. Instead of helping to heal the hurts, dwelling on the past reopens the wounds and intensifies the pain. Remember, if you hope to restore a deteriorating relationship to cooperation, you must be willing to forgive the mistakes of the past.

The Key to Restoration

Russ Johnston is a close friend of mine, author, businessman, and internationally known speaker. One day while we were discussing our weaknesses in solving relationship problems he said, "The problem most of us have is that our own stupidity gets us in trouble and then we are stupid enough to think our own stupidity can get us out, rather than trust God for help!"

I have never forgotten Russ' phrasing of that important truth as it applies to restoring relationships. We need God's help in restoring our relationships. We must confess that we have created our problems by violating God's principles for relationships. The key to restoring those relationships is to begin applying God's principles for human contact and conduct.

Unfortunately, as Russ pointed out, many of us would rather try to solve our problems than rely on God for help. We tend to think, "I got myself into this, so I have to get myself out!" Even though I am a slow learner and often make mistakes, God has been teaching me that His Word provides principles that are far better than I or the world can invent. Following His formula for restoring relationships is the secret to turning around floundering relationships into fulfilling ones.

The Restoration Process

Just as God established universal laws that govern His physical creation enabling us to exist and interact in harmony, He also instituted relational principles enabling us to live peacefully. Defying the laws that govern relationships is just as devastating as ignoring the law of gravity.

All of God's laws are designed for our benefit and good. He

created them so that we might experience peace and happiness. They are the means by which we find fulfillment in life. When we ignore God's laws we quickly discover the negative impact and suffer the serious consequences.

Relationship problems occur as a result of violating one of God's principles for relationships. As long as His laws are obeyed we will experience productive and rewarding relationships. But to reject His rules only causes hurt and heartache. Therefore, as we consider the restoration process we will focus on biblical principles that enable us to reestablish the beneficial relationships that God intended.

Restoring a relationship is a "process." At times it can be a very long process, depending on how far the relationship has deteriorated. Relationships that have been decaying for years can't be restored overnight. Just as it takes time for the body to heal from a serious wound, so it takes time for our emotions to be restored to normal. However, if we faithfully apply the biblical process for restoring relationships we will discover that there is no problem that can't be solved, no hurt that can't be healed. This process is marked by some basic yet crucial components:

▶ Recognize the need for the relationship (Ecc. 4:9-12).
▶ Admit your contribution to the problem (Matt. 7:3-5 and James 5:16).
▶ Ask for forgiveness (Col. 3:12-13 and Matt. 6:14-15).
▶ Decide to put the other person's needs first (Phil. 2:3-4).
▶ Begin "acting out" the qualities of love (1 Cor. 13:4-8).
▶ Decide to focus on the positive (Phil. 4:8).
▶ Trust God for help instead of self (Jer. 17:5-8).

Before we look at the above steps I must again emphasize that the road to restoration is not always an easy one, especially when the relationship is in domination or isolation. It is much easier to destroy a relationship than it is to rebuild one. There are no shortcuts or simple, easy solutions. If there were we wouldn't see so many marriages ending in the divorce courts. However, if all involved in the relationship will commit to applying these seven steps, the relationship, no matter the stage of degeneration, cannot only be restored to cooperation, but it can become stronger than before.

However, one person can't restore the relationship alone. Just as one person isn't fully to blame for the erosion of the relationship, so neither can one person rebuild it. To create hope for hurting relationships everyone in the situation must be willing to commit to take the seven steps.

Recognize the Need for the Relationship

The road back to cooperation always begins by recognizing the need for the relationship. An "I'm sorry" will not solve the problems and restore the relationship. Most people say, "I'm sorry," even when they are walking out of the courtroom following a divorce. Apologizing certainly is an important step in the restoration process, but it isn't the first step. First we must recognize the need for the relationship.

In discerning the need for the relationship we should focus on the following points:

▶ Identify why you need the relationship.
▶ Verbalize the reasons.

Identify why you need the relationship. It isn't enough to say, "I have a need for this relationship." We must clearly identify *why* we need the relationship. It is very difficult to rebuild a deteriorating relationship unless we clearly understand why there is a need for it in the first place.

In looking at the need for relationships we must focus on current needs. We must answer the question: "Why is there a need for this relationship today?" You will probably discover that there are new needs that have developed since the relationship first began.

Ecclesiastes 4:9 tells us, "Two are better than one, because they have a good return for their work." This verse tells us of the need for people to relate together to be more productive.

In reading the following three verses we discover specific needs met by people forming relationships. In verse 10 helping each other in times of need is a reason for forming them. In verse 11 we learn that a relationship can bring warmth and comfort. And in verse 12 we find out that people in the relationship can defend and protect one another. They are stronger together than alone.

Ecclesiastes 4:9-12 is an important passage for relationships because it not only states the need for them, but gives specific benefits of them. This is the starting place for restoring a relationship to cooperation. You must first identify the current need for the relationship. Unless all of the parties involved understand their need for the relationship it will be difficult to navigate the path of restoration. However, identifying individual needs in the relationship provides the purpose and motivation to follow the rest of the steps in returning to cooperation.

Verbalize the reasons. Once current needs have been identified one must be willing to verbalize those reasons to the other member(s) within that relationship. This is extremely important because each person must clearly understand why the relationship is important to the other. As one continues through the steps of restoration, these reasons must remain clearly in focus. Those involved must remind one another of their value and importance.

Those in the latter stages of domination or isolation may discover that the only thing that keeps them moving toward reconciliation is the continual reminder of the relationship's value. Verbalizing to one another the reasons why the relationship is important is often the spark needed to carry on to the next step. This communication cue is crucial to the on-going success of the restoration process.

Admit Your Contribution to the Problem

Once you have identified and verbalized the relationship's importance, the next step is to admit your contribution to the problem. Up to this point people often identify and focus on the weaknesses of the other individual in the relationship. However, trying to restore the relationship by pointing out the other person's problems will only make things worse.

Realizing our tendency to see fault in others while overlooking our own, Jesus said in the Sermon on the Mount:

Why do you look at the speck of sawdust in your brother's eye and pay no attention to the plank in your own eye? How can you say to your brother, "Let me take the speck out of your eye," when all the time there is a plank in your own eye? You hypocrite, first take the plank out of your own eye, and then you will see clearly to remove the speck from your brother's eye (Matt. 7:3-5).

Jesus knows and understands human nature better than we do ourselves. He taught that we can never resolve our conflicts by pointing out the problems in others. We must first recognize and work with our own problems if we hope to ever restore the relationship. However, that is very hard to do when an unfulfilled need causes us to blame others and accuse them of being the problem in the relationship.

Jesus pointed out in Matthew 7:3-5 that as long as we focus on the other person as the problem we cannot see our own. Until we acknowledge our problems and start dealing with them, we cannot make progress in restoring relationships.

James 5:16 tells us, "Confess your sins to each other and pray for each other so that you may be healed." We should not only be ready to admit our contribution to the problem, but we should be willing to pray for each other as well. One of the best ways to heal the pain that exists in deteriorating relationships is to begin praying for the needs, hurts, and concerns of the other person(s). It is difficult to remain angry when you are praying for others' best interests.

Ask for Forgiveness
A few days after Henry fixed my fishing rod we went fishing again. On the way to the mountain stream Henry thanked me for trying to help solve their problems. When I asked him if he was ready to seek her forgiveness he said, "Ask her to forgive me! Why, Myron, she should be asking me to forgive her. I'm not the one giving people the silent treatment, she is."

Henry's attitude is typical of most of our reactions when faced with relationship problems. We tend to feel the other person should be asking for forgiveness, instead of ourselves, because we see the other as the problem. That is why it is important to identify our own contribution to the eroding relationship and focus on that instead of looking at the problems and weaknesses of the other person.

We can't control what the other person does; however, we certainly can control what we do. As long as you wait for the other person to ask for forgiveness there probably isn't much hope for your hurting relationship. Notice what Colossians 3:12-13 tells us, "Therefore, as God's chosen people, holy and dearly loved, clothe yourselves with compassion, kindness, humility, gentleness and patience. Bear with each other and forgive whatever grievances you may have against one another. Forgive as the Lord forgave you."

This is a hard passage to apply because our human nature rejects these godly virtues when we have a grievance against another person. Our emotions rise up, wanting to protect and defend "self," and encourage us to strike back instead of forgive.

But notice the passage goes on to say, "Forgive as the Lord forgave you." That is a very important principle pertaining to the restoration of relationships. Since we are to forgive as the Lord forgave us, we must ask ourselves what that means. God forgave us even though we didn't deserve it. Jesus Christ gave His life for us even while we were still disobedient sinners (Rom. 5:8).

This is the approach to forgiveness we must take when restoring relationships. We, like Jesus, must forgive others first. We must forgive even while we are being wronged. We must forgive even before the other person asks to be forgiven. And notice what Jesus said about the results of our willingness to forgive others. "For if you forgive men when they sin against you, your heavenly Father will also forgive you. But if you do not forgive men their sins, your Father will not forgive your sins" (Matt. 6:14-15).

This passage should be all the motivation we need to forgive others, because if we fail God says He will not forgive us. What a terrible price to pay for letting our pride control us.

As we have already seen in Matthew 5:23-24, when someone has wronged us we aren't to wait for them, we are to initiate the restoration process by asking for their forgiveness. This principle can't be emphasized enough. We must be willing to ask for forgiveness first and mean it, regardless of the reaction of the person we have offended.

Put the Other Person's Needs First

It isn't enough to ask for or offer forgiveness; we must start putting the needs of others ahead of our own. This is often more difficult than asking for forgiveness because it puts actions to our words.

As a relationship degenerates through the various styles people ask for forgiveness many times over. However, they frequently fall right back into their old methods of relating, neglecting the needs of others. As the relationship erodes we tend to no longer believe the person who says, "I'm sorry. Please forgive me."

Therefore, it is extremely important to put action to our words. As soon as we ask for forgiveness we must take the next step and put the needs of others first. This step represents forgiveness in action. It demonstrates to the other person that we mean what we say.

Those who have been operating in a domination or isolation relationship for years are frequently unaware of the real needs of others. That is why it takes a conscious commitment on their part to start meeting the needs of the other person again. It is no longer the natural action it was during the cooperation style relationship.

During this step you will have to get "reacquainted" with the other person in the relationship. Time and effort need to be taken to reopen the lines of communication and reassess the needs of the relationship. You will need all of the virtues of the Colossians 3:12 passage as you begin working on reconciliation. It will take time. Progress will seem slower than you would like. You will fall back into the clutches of self-centeredness from time to time. Mistakes will be made. The other person will not always respond according to your ideals. But whatever you do, don't give up. Apply the biblical principles discussed in this chapter. Your responsibility is to be obedient to what God's Word says and let Him take the responsibility for changing the other person.

Begin Acting Out the Qualities of Love

The next step is to begin "acting out" the qualities of love as presented in 1 Corinthians 13:4-8. Once we start moving away from a cooperation style we tend to act and react more out of emotion. We allow our feelings to dominate our actions. And since our unfulfilled needs tend to generate negative feelings toward the other person we usually act more out of selfishness than love.

Selfishness is the opposite of love. Selfishness draws attention to "me" while love places the focus of attention on the other. First Corinthians 13:4-8 tells us that love is patient, kind, does not envy, does not boast, is not proud, is not rude, is not self-seeking, is not easily angered, doesn't keep a record of wrongs, doesn't delight in evil, is happy with the truth, always protects, trusts, hopes, perseveres, and never fails. When we are experiencing the pain of a degenerating relationship, we don't feel like treating the others with the love described in this passage. In fact, we want to treat them just the opposite.

Therefore, we must force ourselves, against our emotions, to begin practicing love. We must be patient even when all within us is in a hurry. When all of our emotions are telling us to be rude, we must be polite. We must not be self-seeking even when our emotions cry out to focus on "me." No records or score can be kept when we are wronged, even though every emotion in us is pleading to get even. In other words, we do the things love is and "act out" the reality of love as described in this passage, even when we don't want to or feel like it.

Love is action, not just feeling. Love is acting in the best interest of the other person. If you want to rebuild a relationship you must act out love. By the time you reach a domination or isolation relationship there is little "feeling" of love left. However, you must live out love to restore the relationship to cooperation. As you "act out" love you will once again start to develop the emotional feelings that accompany it.

Focus on the Positive

By the time one reaches the bitter stages of the relational styles one tends to spend more time dwelling on the things that are wrong than thinking about the positive and the good.

A relationship can never be rebuilt as long as one focuses on its negative aspects. You must begin redirecting your thoughts to the positive and good qualities. Notice what Philippians 4:8 challenges us to do. "Finally, brothers, whatever is true, whatever is noble, whatever is right, whatever is pure, whatever is lovely, whatever is admirable—if anything is excellent or praiseworthy—think about such things."

Always remember: *Negative attitudes never produce positive actions.* People wind up in divorce courts by dwelling on the negative aspects of their marriage, not because they have been filling their minds with positive things about their spouse.

We all have weaknesses. We all make mistakes. None of us are perfect. The best way I know to undermine a good relationship is by focusing on those negative aspects of the other individual. On the other hand, all of us have just as many strengths as we do weaknesses. Never let yourself be deceived into believing there is nothing positive to focus on in the relationship. There is always as much positive as there is negative, no matter how bad you "feel" the relationship is. If you want to restore what you had during the cooperation relationship style you must begin now focusing on the positive and disregarding the negative.

Trust God for Help

The most important step in restoring a relationship is to learn to trust God instead of relying on one's own emotions and strength. We destroy relationships by violating God's relationship principles. Therefore, in order to restore those relationships we must reinstitute His principles.

Jeremiah 17:5-8 provides an excellent comparison of the person who follows human thoughts and opinions with the individual who follows God's principles. The passage clearly points out that when we follow our own ideas and try to accomplish things in our power, we gain very little. On the other hand, when we follow God's principles and rely on His power, we are highly productive.

This passage warns us not to try to solve our problems by our own strength. God, who made us, also designed and set in motion the relationship principles that will make us the most productive and fulfilled. If we want the best relationships possible we should follow the Creator's designs and not our creaturely emotions.

As you travel back along the path to a cooperation relationship there will be many times when you will say to yourself (and maybe the other person in the relationship), *"I just can't go on! It is no use, I just can't do it!"* More than likely that will be true. You may not be able to do it. That's why we need to rely on God and His power instead of our own.

Notice what Jesus said in Matthew 19:26. "With man this is impossible, but with God all things are possible." Isn't that exciting? The things that are impossible with man are always possible with God. In Genesis 18:14 God asks the question, "Is anything too hard for the Lord?" and in Jeremiah 32:17 we find Jeremiah acknowledging, "Ah, Sovereign Lord, You have made the heavens and the earth by Your great power and outstretched arm. Nothing is too hard for You." The great and powerful God who made the heavens and earth certainly has the power to solve our relationship problems, no matter how big and impossible they may seem to us.

However, God never forces Himself on us against our will. We must invite Him to help us solve our problems. And when we do, notice what He promises us in Jeremiah 33:3. "Call to Me and I will answer you and tell you great and unsearchable things you do not know." In our time of need and trouble God asks us to call upon Him and promises to provide the answers. In Psalm 32:8 He pledges, "I will instruct you and teach you in the way you should go; I will counsel you and watch over you."

Yes, God has the power to solve our problems, but He wants us to invite His help. And when we do He will instruct, teach, and counsel us in His ways. The issue isn't whether God can solve our problems, it is whether we will let Him.

COMMUNICATION: HOW TO SHARE YOUR TRUE SELF

8

Never before in history has humankind had such sophisticated means of communication at its disposal. As a result of advanced technology, men on the moon are able to carry on conversations with men on earth, and unmanned spaceships far out in space can maintain communication with research centers on earth. During the past few years our ability to compile, store, and transmit information has increased at an astronomical rate. However, ironic as it may seem, we have made little, if any, progress in our ability to communicate person to person in our relationships. We are rapidly becoming experts at feeding information into our home computers and retrieving it at the push of a button, but most of us are grossly inept at honestly revealing our thoughts and feelings to another person.

The last time I saw Ed and Jaylene Parker was when I helped them load a U-Haul for their move to California. As we placed their heavy dresser in the truck Ed turned to me and said, "You know, Myron, I've been married to Jaylene for seven years and I'm just now discovering that I don't really know her. I thought we were both happy teaching school and that we would retire in Kansas City the way our folks did. We were going to put our roots down in that community and make a contribution to the educational system there. I guess I thought a lot of things that Jaylene wasn't thinking."

During our lunch break Jaylene said, "I'm so glad to be getting away from the Midwest and out of teaching. Frankly, I thought for a while we were going to rot in that overgrown cow town like both our parents did." Ed glanced at Jaylene and then at me. He had a shocked look on his face as he said, "But I thought you liked teaching and being close to our parents. I thought you were happy with our life there." He took a drink of his Coke and continued, "We were planning to buy a house this fall when we went back to our jobs in the city."

Jaylene smirked and shook her head. "Ed, that's the trouble with you. You don't listen to me. You've never listened to me. I've told you for years we would starve to death teaching school, and it's like I always thought, you didn't hear a word I was saying."

Defining Communication

We all are aware of the need for "good communication" within our relationships; however, some of us have a hard time explaining what we actually mean by the phrase. It was obvious Ed and Jaylene had talked about their situation in Kansas City many times during their time there. However, it was just as clear they hadn't been communicating effectively.

Communication consists of far more than just talking. It is *the process we go through to convey understanding from one person or group to another.* The key word in that definition is "understanding." Unless understanding occurs, we haven't actually communicated. Communication also involves a "process." The goal, or purpose of that process is to convey understanding.

The Communication Process

In defining communication we called it "a process." Therefore, it is important for us to understand the nature of the process:

▶ Step One: Clearly identify the idea and/or feeling to be communicated.

▶ Step Two: Choose the right words and actions to convey the idea and/or feeling.

▶ Step Three: Recognize the barriers in the way of developing understanding.

▶ Step Four: The other person receives our ideas and/or

feelings by listening to our words and observing our actions.

▶ Step Five: The other person translates what is heard and observed.

▶ Step Six: The other person develops an idea and/or feeling based on a correct translation of our words and actions.

When real communication occurs, step one and step six are the same. That is, the person receiving the message winds up understanding the same idea or feeling you were trying to send. Let's look at each of these steps individually and see how the communication process unfolds.

Step One: Clearly identify the idea and/or feeling to be communicated. When we communicate an idea or feeling, we are communicating part of ourselves. And therein lies the first of many problems we encounter when attempting to communicate with others. If I tell you how I really feel and you reject my sentiments, you have rejected a part of me. How many of us get up each morning with the purpose of seeing how many times we can be rejected each day?

Humans awaken each morning with the need to be accepted, not rejected. Therefore, instead of telling people what we actually think and feel, we often tell them only as much about ourselves as we believe they will accept. We do this because we don't want to be rejected.

We will talk more about this later in the chapter; however, at this point it is important that we understand that the first step in the communication process is to identify the ideas or feelings we wish to communicate. If we expect to develop true understanding with others we must be open and honest in sharing those ideas and feelings.

Step Two: Choose the right words and actions to convey the idea and/or feeling. Once we have in mind what we want to communicate, the next step is to choose the proper channels for conveying our ideas or feelings.

However, this poses still another potential problem in the communication process. For example, in the English language

109

the same word may have numerous meanings. Take the word "strike," a very common word. A strike to a bowler is not the same thing as a strike to a baseball player. We strike a match and unions will call a strike, but the same word has totally different meanings, depending on how we use it.

Therefore, in communicating to others, it is very important that they attach the same meaning to your words as you do. Unfortunately, as figure 6 points out, the words we use only convey approximately 7 percent of the complete message. The other 93 percent is transmitted either nonverbally or by tone of voice. This means that most of our communication is done nonverbally. Therefore, the wise listener must learn to discern the true meaning hidden behind the words—the nonverbal communication.

HOW UNDERSTANDING OCCURS

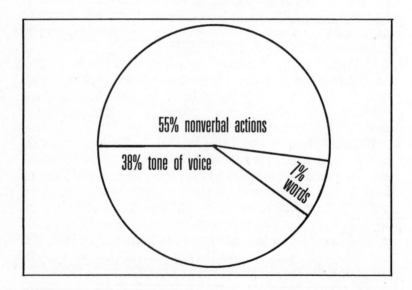

FIGURE 6: This diagram shows the various ways information is communicated. What we say may not be nearly as important as the way we say it.

Step Three: Recognize the barriers in the way of developing understanding. To communicate effectively we must recognize the barriers between the sender of the message and the receiver. A communication barrier is anything that hinders or distorts understanding between the sender and receiver.

To illustrate, it's a fact that our prejudices tend to distort understanding. Interruptions can become major communication barriers. Children playing, a TV blaring, and the phone ringing are all effective interruptions. As we move further away from cooperation, more barriers to effective communication develop. The pain of past hurts prejudices our thinking and we jump to conclusions, hearing before we take the time to listen. For this reason it becomes harder to maintain good communication once the relationship begins degenerating. And the closer we get to isolation, the more difficult communication becomes because of the barriers we have erected.

To develop effective communication we must begin destroying the barriers that stand in our way. We must identify and remove them before real understanding can occur. As long as our communication barriers remain we will always experience misunderstanding. A relationship can never remain in a cooperation style as long as there is excessive misunderstanding.

Step Four: The other person receives our ideas and/or feelings by listening to our words and observing our actions. We noted earlier the important role that nonverbal communication plays. Therefore, the receiver must not only listen to the words being said, but for the meaning and message behind them being conveyed through tone of voice, expressions, and gestures.

As you can see the listener plays a very important role in the communication process. In fact, unless a person is a good listener, understanding cannot occur. It is the responsibility of the listener to "hear the rest of the story" that is transmitted through nonverbal means. Unless a person is able to "listen" in this special way, it will be totally impossible for understanding to occur.

Step Five: The other person translates what is heard and

observed. Once the listener observes the actions (nonverbal communication) and listens to the words of the other, he or she must then translate their meaning.

Step Six: The other person develops an idea and/or feeling based on a correct translation of our words and actions. The end result of the translation process is that the listener develops an idea or feeling. If understanding has actually occurred, step one and step six will be the same. That is, the idea or feeling the sender transmits will be the same as the one the receiver translates, based on the words heard and actions observed.

Trust: A Major Key to Developing Understanding

Trust plays a very important role in the communication process. As we saw in step one above, none of us enjoy being rejected; therefore, we only reveal as much of our true thoughts and feelings as we trust the other person to accept. The more we trust a person the more we are willing to reveal our emotions. The less we trust the other person in the relationship, the less willing we are to open ourselves.

Mistrust closes the door on communication and understanding, pushes people out of our lives, and eventually causes them to begin mistrusting in return. Thus, it is extremely important for people to build their relationships on a strong foundation of trust. You cannot develop and maintain honest communication without it.

For people to be able to share their deepest and most important needs with other people in relationships it is imperative that they trust one another. The more they accept and meet one another's needs, the stronger that trust will be. The stronger the trust, the more willing they will be to open up their lives and share deeper needs and feelings. Trust is one of the major building blocks we use to develop open and honest understanding.

The Goal in Communication: Learning to Be Transparent

As a relationship becomes more meaningful it is important for those in it to learn to be transparent with one another. Transparency means developing such a strong bond of trust that there is liberty to share any thought or feeling without fear of rejection by the other person.

People in such relationships are free to communicate on "the deepest level." They have discovered that communication is not the goal, it is simply a means to an end. Communication is the vehicle through which they encourage, promote, and share the creative potential of one another's personalities.

Transparency does not come easily, but it is the product of hard work. It involves a number of commitments:

▶ Accept the other person as is.
▶ Agree to disagree.
▶ Commit to honesty.
▶ Commit to keeping personal matters in strict confidence.
▶ Agree that nothing is "off limits" to discuss.
▶ Commit to not using privileged information against one another.

Accept the other person as is. This is extremely important because acceptance of one another helps develop the security necessary for transparency to develop.

In far too many relationships people spend most of their time trying to change each other. This communicates rejection and causes withdrawal instead of transparency. It also creates resentment, insecurity, and hostility that erode communication and destroy the relationship.

Accepting the other person doesn't mean approval of everything the individual does. However, you must communicate to the other person your unconditional acceptance of their right to be who they are.

That doesn't mean you avoid troublesome issues. But your acceptance of the person is unconditional. This is the first important step in the development of transparency.

Agree to disagree. Henry Burmeister once told me, "The problem with Maggie is she doesn't have thick enough skin. If you disagree with anything she says she clams up and sometimes won't talk for days. So if I want to avoid the silent

113

treatment I have to go along with her whether I agree or not."

Unfortunately, Maggie is like many others. They haven't learned that it's OK, in fact, frequently healthy, for the relationship to have disagreement. Many people feel threatened when someone in the relationship disagrees with them. They take it personally, feeling that they and not simply their ideas are being rejected.

When people disagree with us it doesn't mean they are rejecting us. Differing viewpoints are healthy for a relationship, because without them we become ingrown and narrow in our thinking.

We should all be willing to agree to disagree. It provides everyone in the relationship with freedom of expression. It makes disagreement acceptable and promotes honesty. There is little hope for the free exchange of ideas when agreement is nothing more than a bargain struck to keep peace. Transparency is out of the question until those involved agree to disagree.

Commit to honesty. A commitment to honesty is important in the development of good communication. Honesty not only builds trust and respect, it does away with suspicion, fear, and doubt, all barriers to open and effective communication. A commitment to honesty provides a framework within which people have the freedom to express and share their innermost selves. Honesty provides the basis for the trust that is so necessary to sharing of the true self with others.

Commit to keeping personal matters in strict confidence. Recently I met a friend of mine in the parking lot at a local mall. We hadn't seen each other in some time so we talked about the latest news in our lives.

During our conversation my friend told me he was in the process of buying out his partner. When I asked him what his wife thought of his prospects he replied, "Oh, she doesn't know yet. If I told her it would be all over town by tomorrow night, and we're wanting to keep it quiet until the deal is finalized."

As I drove out of the parking lot I couldn't help but feel

sorry for my friend. He was very excited but felt he couldn't discuss it with his wife because he couldn't trust her.

If we want people to be open and transparent with us we have to be willing to keep those things in confidence that aren't for general public knowledge. Unless we are willing to make such a commitment we will never be able to develop and maintain a significant depth of sharing.

Agree that nothing is "off limits" to discuss. I have met couples married for over twenty years who never had a good sexual relationship because they were unwilling to discuss their sexual needs. To develop a rewarding relationship with your mate, you must be willing to discuss anything. You need to develop a ground rule that encourages discussing any topic of importance. Nothing should be considered off limits as long as you agree to keep appropriate information in strict confidence.

Commit to not using privileged information against one another. When we become transparent we also become vulnerable. People know our deepest secrets, greatest strengths, most serious weaknesses, and our highest hopes and expectations. They know more about us than any other. This is a great experience and a level of communication that few people are willing to develop. It is a great honor to have another person share that much of themselves with you. Whatever you do, don't take advantage of that person's trust in you by ever using that information against them.

Actions Speak Louder than Words

The old saying, "Actions speak louder than words," certainly applies to communication in our personal relationships. Most of the time what we are doing speaks so loud people can't even hear what we are saying. Our actions reveal our thoughts far more than our words. If people want to know what you think of them, all they have to do is watch how you treat them. Your actions reveal more truth about your feelings than what you say.

Much confusion occurs as a result of the misunderstanding

of actions. In many instances we say one thing, but our actions contradict our words. Contradictions between words and actions always lead to confusion and mistrust. People will ultimately believe our actions instead of our words. When our actions constantly belie our words we give others no reason to keep faith in us.

To be an effective communicator make sure your actions and words are telling the same story. Love in action means not saying what you do, but doing what you say.

TAKING THE FIGHT OUT OF CONFLICT

9

Conflict can be defined as *open and hostile opposition that occurs as a result of opposing viewpoints.* Conflict is different and much more serious than disagreement. Conflict *always* involves "hostility."

Disagreement is healthy and usually beneficial to a relationship; however, conflict is extremely unhealthy and almost always detrimental. A disagreement can be elevated to the level of conflict simply by adding the element of hostility, while a conflict can be diminished to the level of disagreement by removing the element of hostility.

In facing conflict the goal is to first remove the hostility and diminish it to a disagreement, because as long as hostility is present it is almost impossible to arrive at solutions.

The greater the level of hostility, the more difficult it is to reach an agreeable solution. Hostility causes an individual to act emotionally and greatly impairs one's ability to operate rationally. Anger causes us to do and say things we would never dream of were we not being controlled by this dangerous emotion.

The Cause of Conflict

Conflict occurs as a result of pent-up hostility produced when people's perceived needs are not being met. When the need has enough importance attached to it, people are easily hurt when that need is not met. Hostility must always have a target. We either become angry at ourselves or at the person causing the hurt. Conflict occurs when we release our anger on the person

117

we deem responsible for our emotional pains.

Conflict is usually the result of opposing views. Each person claims the right to infallibility. People involved in conflict are in a struggle for control. They want to dominate the situation so their needs will be met. During the conflict those involved see it as a "win/lose situation." There is no compromise. This attitude causes the conflict to intensify, because each is committed to winning at the other's expense. They believe they are justified in taking whatever action necessary to win the struggle for control.

The Negative Results of Conflict

Continued conflict is usually destructive to relationships. Conflict regularly produces the following negative results:

► It causes us to magnify the weaknesses in others.
► It leads us to a self-centered attitude.
► It weakens and often destroys our trust in others.
► It may break up the relationship.

It causes us to magnify the weaknesses in others. Janice and Charles Stone's conflict over David's living situation degenerated to where they were doing everything possible to discredit each other.

At one point Charles said, "If you aren't cooking any better now than when we were married, poor David is probably starving to death. You couldn't even fry chicken." Later in their screaming match Janice blasted Charles by saying, "You always did have to be the center of attention! You couldn't even put your coat on in public without making it a major production."

Obviously the way one cooked chicken or put on a coat in public had nothing to do with their son's situation. These were statements designed to emphasize the faults in the other person, a natural result occurring in the heated battle of conflict.

Galatians 5:15 says, "If you keep on biting and devouring each other, watch out or you will be destroyed by each other." This provides an accurate description of the evolution of conflict. We fight one another, fabricate other's faults, and try to devour the other by discrediting them. In the process the relationship is frequently destroyed.

It leads us to a self-centered attitude. Those involved in conflict tend to become more and more self-centered. As a result they move further away from a cooperation relationship style. As self-centeredness increases we forget the needs of others. And so the pattern continues, as needs are neglected the relationship degenerates into isolation or termination.

It weakens, and often destroys our trust in others. While Janice, Charles, and I were talking one day, she turned to him and said, "You want David to live with you so you can turn him against me. I lost a husband and now you want to take my son! Next you'll be trying to take my daughter away from me! Haven't you hurt me enough? Why don't you go away and leave us alone?"

Janice no longer trusted Charles' motives. She was convinced he wanted to turn David against her. This type of mistrust faithfully accompanies conflict. As long as people in conflict mistrust one another, workable solutions are difficult to reach.

It may break up the relationship. The longer conflict goes unresolved the greater damage to a relationship. Notice the Apostle Paul's specific teaching on this topic. "If you are angry, don't sin by nursing your grudge. Don't let the sun go down with you still angry—get over it quickly; for when you are angry you give a mighty foothold to the devil" (Eph. 4:26-27, TLB). This passage makes it clear that conflict should be resolved as quickly as possible. We are not to let the day end mired in a conflict. Such casual attitudes create an atmosphere ripe for wrecking relationships.

The Value of Disagreements

Unlike conflict, disagreement can be very beneficial to relationships. There are two particular positive aspects of disagreement:

▶ It can lead to personal growth.

▶ It can help us become more tolerant of opposing views.

It can lead to personal growth. Disagreement can lead to personal growth by causing us to see the need for change. Proverbs 27:17 says, "As iron sharpens iron, so one man sharpens another." The element of opposing views is very healthy and beneficial as long as it doesn't create hostility. Facing different views can cause awareness of the need to change leading to the individual's personal growth.

It can help us become more tolerant of opposing views. Disagreement helps those in a relationship learn to be flexible and realize that "my" way is not the "only" way. It helps us to be more accepting of others and willing to change as needed. Further, it helps us avoid rigid structures that can lead to stagnation in the relationship.

Removing the Hostility from a Conflict

It is difficult to resolve conflict where hostility is present, because it tends to impair one's ability to think objectively. Therefore, in dealing with conflict the first step is to remove the hostility. This is accomplished by changing the goal of the conflict from that of "win/lose" to "win/win."

The win/lose approach to a conflict fosters humility. As long as those involved think someone is going to win and someone will lose they aggressively vie for victory.

In order to remove hostility you must take a win/win approach to conflict. That means arriving at a workable solution satisfactory to everyone involved. The win/win approach takes the fight out of the conflict. It removes the need to struggle for control. If you fail to take a win/win approach to your conflicts, then eventually everyone will lose, because there is not such a thing as a win/lose solution to conflict within relationships.

When we take a win/lose approach to conflict resolution the first time loser is determined to be the next time winner, because we all hate to lose. This immediately sets up those involved for a repeat performance as soon as the first conflict is over. Each subsequent conflict moves the relationship further away from a spirit of cooperation until eventually everyone loses.

Resolving Conflicts Using a "Win/Win" Approach

To resolve conflict using a win/win approach those in the relationship must go through the following steps:

▶ Identify the real needs and issues.
▶ Sort out facts from feelings.
▶ Agree to find solutions satisfactory to all.
▶ Identify the various options available.
▶ Choose the option that most fully meets the needs of all involved.

Identify the real needs and issues. This is the first step in a win/win approach to conflict resolution. It seems obvious, but when we are involved in the heat of conflict we usually lose our objectivity.

For example, after Janice and Charles agreed to try the win/win approach, I asked them to define the real issues for me. Janice looked at me like I was out of my mind and said, "Myron, surely you've been listening to us for the last two hours, haven't you? The issue is whether David is going to live with me or Charles!" Before I could respond Charles replied, "I'm not so sure about that. In fact, that shouldn't be the issue at all. The real issue is what is best for David."

There was a long silence and then I asked Janice what she thought about Charles' statement. "Well, actually he's right," she admitted. Eventually Janice and Charles realized how they had been acting, neglecting to focus on what was best for David. They had been caught in a web of selfishness.

It is easy to lose sight of the real issues during the midst of conflict, especially when the problem is approached from a win/lose position. Thus, it is necessary to agree on the real issues of focus, instead of personal emotional concerns.

After a while both Janice and Charles looked at me and he said, "Well, now that we know what the real issue is, what's next? Where do we go from here?"

Sort out facts from feelings. It is easy to get so caught up in our feelings that we lose sight of the facts. I suggested to the Stones that they objectively discuss the real issue, being honest about their personal situations as they related to David.

There was another long silence and finally Janice said, "The facts are David wants to live with his dad. He and his sister don't get along together. He is becoming very hostile toward me and it's getting harder to control him." She took a deep breath and continued, "I don't want David to live with his dad, because I'd miss him and because I want revenge from Charles!"

Time must be spent sorting out facts from feelings. There is no replacement for this investment. Only when the facts are clear can we move on to the next step.

Agree to finding solutions satisfactory to all. This is an important step because it removes the fear of being forced into a decision. It takes the pressure off and frees people up to focus their efforts and energies on finding the best solutions.

Identify the various options available. Janice and Charles spent a considerable amount of time identifying and discussing the various options available. It is crucial that people in conflict don't latch onto the first option for convenience sake. A win/win situation occurs only when all options have been explored and the one best suited for the situation is chosen. Take all the time you need during this step of conflict resolution.

Choose the option that most fully meets the needs of all involved. Finally, Janice and Charles reached a decision. David would spend the school year with Charles and the following summer with Janice. At that time they would meet again to evaluate that arrangement.

This is one example of a couple who worked through their hostilities by focusing on a win/win approach instead of the win/lose method. In the process they realized that they must learn to work together for there would be future conflict situations that would demand the same disciplined approach.

Ground Rules when Dealing with a Conflict
There are several guidelines we must follow in order to successfully deal with a conflict. These six ground rules play an

important role in successfully dealing with conflict. By following these simple rules you will have less difficulty when dealing with disagreements.

▶ Always attack the problem, never the person.
▶ Always verbalize feelings, never act them out.
▶ Forgive instead of judging the other person.
▶ Be committed to giving more than you take.
▶ Don't just talk, make understanding your aim.
▶ When the conflict is over put it behind you.

Always attack the problem, never the person. This is a very difficult rule to follow, especially when one is angry. When you attack a person you only intensify the hostility of that individual. As the enmity is increased within the conflict it becomes more difficult to arrive at a workable solution. When you attack the individual as being the problem, you force that person to become defensive. In all probability they will in turn attack, blaming you.

Make sure you keep your focus on the problem instead of the person. You can solve problems much easier than you can change people. The person may have caused the problem, but he or she is not the problem. Make sure you always make that distinction. You will discover conflicts are much easier to solve.

Always verbalize feelings, never act them out. If you are angry, say so! Don't pout and contain your frustrations. You will find it is far less offensive to state your feelings than to act them out. This is especially true during the tension-charged environment of a conflict.

Forgive instead of judging the other person. Never approach conflict for the purpose of establishing yourself as the judge and jury in determining right and wrong. The issue isn't who is right and wrong, it's what is the solution to the problem. Your job is to forgive the other person who has offended you and let the individual know you are interested only in solving the problem, not establishing their guilt.

Be committed to giving more than you take. This is a very difficult rule to follow when dealing with conflicts; however, I can assure you that it is one of the most important. Luke 6:38 tells us, "Give, and it will be given to you. A good measure, pressed down, shaken together and running over, will be poured into your lap." And in Matthew 5:40-41 Jesus said, "And if someone wants to sue you and take your tunic, let him have your cloak as well. If someone forces you to go one mile, go with him two miles."

In these passages we discover a key principle for facing conflict. First, in Luke we are told that if we give we will get more back in return. Then in Matthew Jesus is telling us to do more than is required of us. Even though these are hard rules to follow in the midst of a conflict, God promises that if we are faithful He will be with us.

Don't just talk, make understanding your aim. During a conflict it is easy to talk a lot and say very little. We must be reminded that we will never solve the problems until we correctly understand what they are. Deal with problems head-on and make "understanding" them the objective of all your conversations.

When the conflict is over put it behind you. There is nothing worse than constantly reminding someone of their contribution to a problem. When the problem is solved put it behind you and don't keep bringing it up. Dwelling on past problems is the fastest way I know of insuring new ones in the future. Nothing is gained by focusing on past mistakes and problems.

Be Committed to Learn from Your Mistakes

None of us enjoy conflicts but from time to time all of us have to work our way through them. Even though it is hard to see the good in them, we must realize that conflicts can be beneficial.

James 1:2-4 tells us, "Consider it pure joy, my brothers, whenever you face trials of many kinds, because you know that the testing of your faith develops perseverance. Perseverance must finish its work so that you may be mature and complete, not lacking anything." Notice the principles in this passage. First, we are told to have a positive attitude when dealing with our problems. This doesn't come naturally for most of us. Instead of being positive when dealing with problems, most of us say, "Why me?" and tend to become negative, and maybe even depressed.

However, as we look deeper into the passage we discover why we need a positive attitude. We learn that our problems help develop us into mature people.

We have one of two options when facing relational problems. We can say, "Woe is me. I feel so sorry for myself. I don't deserve all these problems." Taking that approach, we will meet nothing but frustration. On the other hand, we can say, "I've made a mistake. I have a problem, and I'm going to learn all I can so I won't repeat this mistake again."

If we take this latter approach we will discover the truth presented in James 1:2-4. Our problems are opportunities to learn from mistakes. Our failures can and should be life's best teachers. However, we must be willing to recognize that fact and look for the opportunity to learn and grow when facing them in our relationships.

Always remember, we'll never reach a place in our relationships that will be totally free from conflict. The issue isn't whether we have conflicts in our relationships, it's how we deal with them that counts.

MARRIAGE: PULL TOGETHER OR YOU'LL PULL APART

10

In chapter one I pointed out that there is no such thing as status quo when talking about relationships. A relationship is constantly changing for the better, or for the worse. We are either pulling together to make things better, or we wind up pulling apart. And it is possible to switch sides within the relationship at any time we choose.

It is a choice. We chose to pull together to form a cooperation relationship style. We start pulling apart because we decide to stop trying. At some point in time someone consciously decides to switch sides, stop relating in a cooperation style, and begin pulling in the opposite direction.

In Mark 3:24-25 Jesus said, "If a kingdom is divided against itself, that kingdom cannot stand. If a house is divided against itself, that house cannot stand." This teaching of Jesus not only applies to kingdoms and families, but to all relationships. He is pointing out that division destroys relationships. We must ask ourselves a question: "How can we avoid these destructive divisions?"

We must recognize that there is a great difference between symptoms and an actual illness. We never cure the disease by simply treating the symptoms. A frequent headache is one symptom of high blood pressure. Taking one or two aspirin will make the headache go away. But just treating the symptom won't control the high blood pressure, even though we may temporarily calm the headache.

This analogy applies to treating problems in relationships. We must make sure we are curing the "disease," not just treating the symptoms. I recently heard a minister say, "Divorce is the disease threatening to destroy modern-day society!" That is not true. Divorce is not a disease at all. It is only a symptom of the disease. We will never solve relationship problems by simply avoiding divorce.

Divorce is the end result of long-term unresolved problems. Some of those problems started prior to marriage and were brought into the relationship on the wedding day. Historically, the church has opposed divorce. However, opposing divorce is not the answer, because opposition does not solve the problems that cause it. The church not only needs to oppose divorce, it needs to help people avoid it.

Divorces within Christendom are increasing at about the same rate as in the non-Christian community today. As a result, in recent years many churches have developed "divorce recovery workshops" to help the victims recover. Many people have been helped by workshops. Unfortunately, not nearly enough churches and ministries are conducting "divorce prevention classes," designed to cure or prevent relational problems. Until that happens we will see increasing numbers of people signing up for recovery workshops.

In this chapter we will look specifically at marriage, focusing on how to keep pulling together and examining those factors that help remove division within relationships. In order to maintain unity within relationships we must focus on five key ingredients:

▶ Develop a common purpose for your relationship.
▶ Keep the relationship focused on common goals.
▶ Commit to reviewing progress on goals twice a year.
▶ Support the development of each other's talents and abilities.
▶ Encourage and participate in each other's spiritual growth and potential.

Develop a Common Purpose for Your Relationship

When a friend's marriage falls apart most of us ask ourselves, *"I wonder why they got a divorce?"* Another question needs to be answered. The first question asked should be, *"Why did they get married in the first place?"* Couples considering marriage should honestly face and answer that very important question—why are they getting married?

I have asked many people experiencing marital problems that question and their answers are alarming. Here are some of those answers I have received:

▶ "I got married because I was lonely living by myself."
▶ "All of my friends were getting married and I didn't want to be left behind."
▶ "I wanted to have a family."
▶ "I was pregnant, so we got married."
▶ "My parents thought we should get married."
▶ "Because we were in love!"

None of the above reasons justify getting married. And certainly not just because you are in love. Most who get a divorce were in love when they got married. Just being in love can't be reason enough for marriage.

People should not get married until they first identify the *purpose* for their marriage. Some may say, "We know the purpose, it is to love each other. That's why we want to get married, because we love each other!" Again I say that most everyone who marries says the same thing, and today 50 percent of them are winding up in divorce courts. It takes far more than loving each other to make a marriage work. I know, because one day I said, "I promise to love, honor, and cherish till death do us part," but later became one of those 50 percent who fell victim to divorce.

You must have a clearly defined purpose for marriage. Without one you will find that the feelings you were originally calling "love" may not be strong enough to pull you through the rough places that are ahead.

During my management training seminars and consulting work with organizations I explain that every group must have a purpose, and that is equally true with marriage relationships. Purpose tells *why*. It explains the reason for marriage just as it explains the reason for the existence of an organization. It must be a "common purpose." By that I mean both people in the relationship have worked in developing its purpose. It is a common purpose when both are committed to it. They "own it"; it is theirs. If the purpose is developed by only one of the partners, then the partnership is doomed without a feeling of ownership.

Norman and Susan Plumely spent the first 10 years of their marriage working hard. Norman was an insurance salesman and Susan worked as a dental assistant. They had three children, all girls, and after a few years Norman started his own business as an independent insurance broker. He did very well and soon had a sales staff of 10 people working out of his office.

After the third child Norman insisted that Susan quit her job and stay home with the children. He never had liked her to work and insisted that the husband should be the provider of the family. During those 10 years they moved three times into a larger home. Norman was a good provider; he was able to buy his family almost anything they wanted.

Susan was in charge of children's church and Norman taught an adult Sunday School class. They seemed like the role model of success, both in the secular and Christian community. Everyone who knew them was shocked when they got a divorce.

Susan said, "I got tired of being another one of Norman's possessions. Everything was Norman's. It was his business, farm, horses, and kids. Even the dog belonged to Norman. I was known around the community as Norman's wife!"

Norman was the sole owner of whatever purpose that existed in their marriage. Susan felt she had no involvement in his life or input into their marriage. That was one of the things that pulled them apart. To pull together you must be unified around a purpose for that relationship. Without a clearly defined purpose giving meaning to the relationship, people find it hard to continue their commitments to one another.

The purpose provides the basis for planning your future together. Your purpose tells why you are in a marriage relationship. It defines the "cause" you are committed to in the relationship and it provides the basis for planning your future. Without a clearly defined purpose it is easy to wind up like Norman and Susan. Purpose in a relationship plays the same role as the rudder on a ship, both help in keeping on course in the face of opposition.

Lasting plans in a relationship cannot be made until a common purpose has been determined. Once that is determined, then plans can be developed that will help the relationship achieve its purpose. Always remember: purpose tells why you are in the relationship, and plans show how that purpose can be accomplished.

Keep the Relationship Focused on Common Goals

Just as a relationship needs to have a common purpose, it must also contain common goals. That is, the goals must be jointly developed so that each individual feels ownership of those goals. Plans must be focused on a common goal and help meet common needs.

Susan Plumely told me, "We always had to do what Norman wanted to do. He never asked my opinion. He even made a down payment on a farm before I even knew he was thinking about moving." She continued her description of life with Norman by saying, "I never did like that farm. It was so far from all my friends in town. And it was a major project just to go shopping. But Norman didn't care. He thought more of his horses than he thought of me and my needs!"

Susan and Norman lacked common goals. Norman lived his life, and spent his money in the way that served him best, ignoring Susan in the planning and goal-setting process of the relationship. And as they discovered, that is a sure way to begin pulling a relationship apart at the seams.

Our goals and objectives must be measurable. To be "measurable" means they should tell us the following:

▶ What is to be accomplished.
▶ How it is to be accomplished.
▶ When it will be accomplished.

131

Each person in the relationship should have direct input into these three aspects of determining measurable goals. Susan obviously didn't have an opportunity to give input. I'm sure Norman spent considerable time thinking about their move, but Susan didn't find out until after the deal was sealed. As a result, the decision on the new country home did not meet her needs. In fact, the decision created many problems and frustrations for her, all of which could have been easily avoided if they both had been involved in determining their needs in a new home.

Jointly setting measurable goals and objectives helps insure that more of everyone's needs will be met. It forces those in the relationship to be more specific and make less assumptions. It also makes it easier to evaluate your success in achieving those goals and objectives.

Commit to Reviewing Progress Twice Each Year
It isn't enough to set common goals that are measurable; twice each year a couple needs to review their progress in achieving them. I suggest you take an entire weekend to review your goals. If you have children, hire a baby-sitter or leave them with relatives. You will need an entire weekend to focus on one another and to evaluate the goals of your life together.

When planning for this weekend, if at all possible, look to go out of town. If you stay at home distractions will interfere and temptations call to interrupt this crucial planning and reviewing time. Don't let it happen.

Pick a place out of town that will allow you to relax and enjoy some recreational time together. Don't give the phone number out to anyone except for emergencies. If at all possible, make arrangements to get there Friday evening and use the first night as an opportunity to go out alone together.

Use both Saturday and Sunday mornings to work on and evaluate your goals for the relationship. Use the afternoons to rest, relax, and play together. As you discuss the goals, make sure you are developing and maintaining balance in both your personal lives as well as the relationship. By that I mean make sure you are dividing your time and energies properly between careers, time for each other and the family, recreational time, and personal growth and development.

Remember, this is a time of evaluation. Therefore, it is extremely important that you are honest with one another and willing to give and accept constructive criticism. This will require your willingness to be objective. This time together should include examining goals in such areas of your life and relationship as:

- ▶ Your spiritual growth and development.
- ▶ Your financial plans.
- ▶ How you spend free time together as a couple and family.
- ▶ Major purchases you plan to make during the next year.
- ▶ Plans for personal growth and development as individuals, a couple, and family during the next year.
- ▶ Development of your sexual relationship.
- ▶ Discussion of major relationship problems and how they will be resolved.

This is only a sample list. You will want to expand upon it according to your personal needs. Remember, you aren't just going to *talk* about these areas of your relationship, you will develop an "action plan" with goals and objectives that can be objectively evaluated to monitor your progress.

People I have encouraged to do this, report that it is a highlight of the year. I think you will agree with me once you begin the process. It is an effective means of helping people in a relationship to pull together, rather than pulling the relationship apart.

Support the Development of Each Other's Talents and Abilities
When people get married they bring to the relationship two sets of talents and abilities. One of the goals of every marriage should be to encourage and support the development of these.

Recently I was in Canada conducting a series of seminars on burnout. Following one of the sessions a young woman approached me and asked if I would sign a book. I excused myself and followed her to the book table. After I autographed her book she asked me if I thought it possible for someone her age to be experiencing burnout.

I found out that she had just completed a master's degree in electronics and was working for a computer manufacturing company. When I asked what her husband did she laughed and said, "Oh, I'm not married." Something about the way she said it led me to believe she was opposed to marriage.

She told me that her mother had been a highly talented and promising concert pianist before marrying her father. She had performed in both London and the United States and many said·she was destined for greatness. However, when she got married, her husband, who was a tax accountant, insisted that she stop performing and raise a family.

The longer she talked, the more bitterness showed in her voice. "My mother plays the piano at church once a week, and that's about all," she said, her voice strained with resentment. "My father doesn't like the piano, so Mom doesn't even play much at home, unless he's gone." She ended by saying, "My father prevented my mother from pursuing a very promising career in music, so I'm sort of turned off with the whole idea of marriage. I've got a lot of things I want to accomplish with my life and I think marriage would hinder them."

I was very frustrated following my conversation with that woman, because unfortunately, in all too many marriages, one or both of the individuals is prevented from developing his or her talents. However, just the opposite should be true. The marriage bond should be the place where individuals can find encouragement and support for developing their gifts.

Marriage should help bring out the best in a person, not destroy one's potential. Bringing out the best in one another helps draw couples closer together instead of further apart. Make supporting each other's development a priority. The goal is to help one another develop those special skills, abilities, and interests to their full potential. People in a marriage relationship are there to encourage one another, not to compete. And the more you encourage one another in the development of special skills, the stronger the relationship will become.

Encourage and Participate in Each Other's Spiritual Growth and Potential

Spiritual development can become a factor in eroding the relationship of one person is interested in growing spiritually and the other one isn't. And unfortunately, all too often that is the case. Even though we should participate in each other's spiritual growth, if one of the individuals is uninterested in spiritual development, it is important that the other person respect those feelings.

We must always remember that Jesus Christ never forced Himself on anyone, and neither should we. If one of the marriage partners is not as interested in spiritual growth as the other, then follow this principle taught in the New Testament. "Wives, fit in with your husbands' plans; for then if they refuse to listen when you talk to them about the Lord, they will be won by your respectful, pure behavior. Your godly lives will speak to them better than any words" (1 Peter 3:1-2, TLB).

This passage tells us that one should never try to push spiritual growth onto his or her mate. Our lives should be so attractive that he or she would also want to become involved in spiritual things.

Assuming that both people in the marriage are interested in spirituality, it is important that each share in the development of the other. Some couples find it more difficult to share in one another's spiritual growth than in each other's personal development. If you are experiencing difficulty, try implementing some of the following suggestions:

▶ Instead of one playing the role of leader or teacher, approach the subject as equals under mutual submission.
▶ Try working through the Book of Proverbs, studying how it applies to the situations you face daily.
▶ Never criticize the ideas or insights your mate receives from a certain passage.
▶ As you read the Bible, look for principles that apply to your family life.
▶ Make a list of individual and mutual prayer requests and share the results with each other.

▶ If you have difficulty in deciding on a study topic, make a trip to your local Christian bookstore and ask for assistance in selecting a daily devotional book.

Even though you may feel a little uncomfortable doing these things at first, you will soon discover that working on your spiritual development together is wonderful medicine for strengthening your relationship. But remember, let each person grow and develop at his or her rate. The important thing isn't how fast you grow spiritually, but that you are consistent and faithful in doing it together.

Work at Becoming a Team

One of the goals of your relationship should be to work at becoming a team, not just two individuals living together in something called a marriage. According to Genesis 2:18, people in a relationship should be "helpers" of one another. And that should be the goal in the marriage relationship; we should be committed to be each other's helpers.

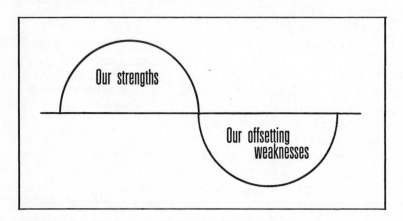

FIGURE 7: Everyone brings to a relationship a set of strengths and offsetting weaknesses.

The goal in marriage, or for any relationship for that mat-

136

ter, is to allow each individual to work in his or her area of strength. However, most of us are so concerned about our weaknesses that we spend too much time trying to minimize them instead of working in our area of strength.

Therefore, the goal, as illustrated in figure 8 below, is to team up to help each other in our respective areas of weakness, so that we can in turn allow each other to concentrate more fully on our areas of strength. As we saw in an earlier chapter, this principle is clearly taught and illustrated in Ecclesiastes 4:9-12.

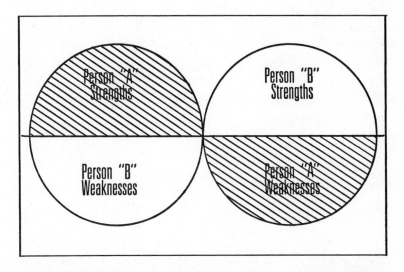

FIGURE 8: When we form a true team we are allowing one person's strengths to compensate for the other individual's weaknesses.

If you want to make sure you are pulling together instead of pulling apart, then team up with each other and help in your areas of weakness, and encourage in your areas of strength. As the Bible points out, you will accomplish far more together than you would alone.

DEALING WITH RELATIONSHIP FAILURE

11

Vern Masterson and I walked slowly up the back trail of Pikes Peak in silence. It was a beautiful, warm summer afternoon, perfect for a hike in the Colorado Rockies. A small snow-fed stream made a funny gurgling sound as it meandered through the moss-covered rocks, dead trees, and tundra-like vegetation that carpeted the floor of this small mountain valley.

We were at about 12,000 feet elevation, our backpacks were beginning to feel like lead, and our lungs were craving more oxygen as we stopped to rest before setting up camp for the weekend. As we slipped our packs off our weary shoulders and leaned them against a large boulder, Vern looked at me and with a contrived smile said, "Are you sure this is the kind of therapy I need? I feel a lot worse than when I got up this morning!"

I had invited Vern to go backpacking for the weekend because the following Monday his divorce would be finalized and having been through the experience, I knew Vern was emotionally upset. He and Hazel had been married almost twenty years. A few months ago Vern came home from a business trip and found a note informing him that Hazel was leaving and filing for divorce.

They had been having marital problems for several years and for the past six months had been seeing a counselor weekly. According to Vern, Hazel had always resented him because they were unable to have children. And as time went by, that resentment became stronger until finally she left him

While Vern set up the tent, I gathered firewood and started

boiling water for coffee. That evening we sat around the camp fire and Vern began to talk, his voice trembling as he said, "I don't know what I'll do without her, Myron. We grew up across the street from one another. I've known Hazel all my life. I don't think I can live without her." He was quiet for a while then said, "One minute I want to get on my knees and beg her to take me back and the next minute I'm so angry I'd like to kill her!"

Words seemed to flow out of Vern like a penned up stream breaking through a dam. We talked late into the night about his feelings of guilt, rejection, anger, and loneliness. Now and then he would inject, "Myron, I don't know what I'm going to do. I don't think life will ever be worth living again."

His feelings were typical. I knew the frustration pent up inside this man. I knew what he was going through, because I had been there. And I had learned what I had been telling him really is true—there is hope for hurting people, even when a relationship as important as a marriage fails.

The Need for This Chapter
During the past ten chapters of this book the emphasis has been on hope for hurting relationships. We have discussed why relationships are formed, how they deteriorate, and how to restore them to cooperation. We have looked at the important role communication plays in developing and maintaining a good relationship. Techniques for dealing with conflict were discussed, and we have explained how to develop the kind of unity that allows people to pull together instead of pulling apart.

However, we must also face some frightening realities. Almost 50 percent of all marriages today are ending in divorce. Not everyone who reads this book will rebuild their hurting relationships, not because the principles aren't true but because they won't have an opportunity. Everyone in the relationship must be committed and willing to apply these principles for them to be effective. Experience teaches that not everyone is.

Some of you reading this book may already be divorced. Some of you may be in the middle of one and others may be on the very edge of divorce. For you, the next two chapters will be particularly helpful. I have been there and I can report that there is also *hope for hurting people* whose world has crashed down around them.

Divorce Versus Physical Death

Divorce is one of the most emotionally devastating experiences a person can go through. In some ways it is worse than the grief one experiences when a loved one dies. When physical death occurs there is the trauma of the funeral and the period of intense grief that follows because of the loss. The body is placed within a grave and a headstone is set to mark the place of interment.

Death also occurs when there is a divorce. The relationship actually "dies." Budding future plans die on the vine. Interaction between people (and sometimes within the entire family) stops. Couples walk away from homes and possessions they spent their entire married lives saving for and accumulating. Friendships are suddenly broken and lost, sometimes forever. Life as they have known it suddenly comes to an end and the courtroom becomes the funeral of the marriage.

However, in divorce the "corpses" still walk around as constant reminders of the marriage's demise. When a loved one dies, they are gone and you don't see them again. But with divorce the pangs of death are just as severe, and frequently more so, because you do see the other person again, and yet you can't resurrect the relationship.

With death the grave is "final." Yet, with a marriage relationship that dies, the separation is not final. In many instances the divorce is never over. The divorce does not necessarily "finalize" the need to relate. For example, when there are children involved, there are frequent phone calls and meetings with the ex-partner to work out the visitation privileges This may go on for years.

Even as the children grow up it isn't over. There are children's weddings to attend (that is, if you are invited). There are often grandchildren to consider and decisions to face about where young ones will spend holidays and vacations. On and on it goes through the remainder of your life.

In many ways divorce is worse than physical death, because with death you no longer deal with the issues that affect the living. But in divorce, even though the relationship dies, you are constantly faced with the issues of life that continue to revolve around the dead relationship.

Is There Life after Divorce?

When a relationship dies, those involved often wish for death because they feel they can no longer face life without the relationship and the world that surrounded it. In fact, almost every divorced person I have talked to has contemplated, at some point in time, suicide. So take heart, if you are experiencing such feelings, you certainly aren't alone. Others, like yourself, have felt the same way.

But I can assure you there is life after divorce! There is a fulfilling life ahead for those individuals who are willing to work through the emotional baggage that results from a divorce. You not only can recover, but you can take hold of the opportunity to become a better person as a consequence of the mistakes and pain you have experienced. The road back to a fulfilling life is a hard one and not everyone is willing to pay the price for restoration.

There is life after divorce; it can be a good life. Those people who fail to experience it do so because they choose to, not because they have to. During the remainder of this chapter we will look at the road to recovery and the full life that can be experienced by those who have gone through a divorce.

The Steps to Recovery

The road to divorce recovery is a complicated and arduous trek as figure 9 indicates. There are many steps in the process. We will begin by looking at the first step—denial—which, ironically, should not be viewed negatively, but rather positively

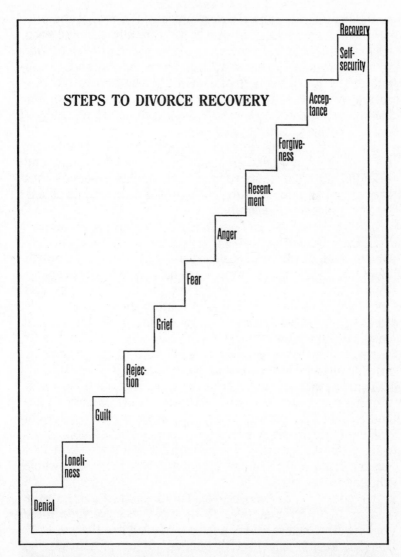

STEPS TO DIVORCE RECOVERY

Recovery

Self-security

Acceptance

Forgiveness

Resentment

Anger

Fear

Grief

Rejection

Guilt

Loneliness

Denial

FIGURE 9: The steps to divorce recovery are a steep, difficult, and long climb; however, there is a full and rewarding life waiting for all who are willing to make the journey.

as the beginning of the recovery process. The rest of the process will then be mapped out as we carefully examine each stage along the road for recovery. *It is important to note that these steps are not necessarily sequential.* People move in and out of the various stages and, in fact, may be experiencing several of them at the same time. One thing is certain: the feelings represented by these steps are common to all navigating their way to recovery.

Some of these steps are much more difficult and take longer to "master" than others. And some of them, such as anger and resentment, often seem to represent similar emotions, but each contains different hurdles that must be overcome as one travels the path to recovery.

Step One: Denial

One of the first feelings people experience when going through divorce is shock. They know divorce happens to other people— their friends, neighbors, and relatives. But no one ever expects it to happen to them. Standing in front of the minister people pledge to the marriage covenant by vowing, "Till death we do part." At that point they believe that only death will ever separate them. People certainly don't take marriage vows by saying, "Till divorce makes us part!"

Thus, we are not only shocked when we find ourselves midst a divorce, but we don't want anyone to know. We ask, "How could this be happening to me?" Divorce represents failure of the most important relationship in our lives. And none of us want to admit, especially to the world, that we failed. At first we try to deny the failure, thinking it will make this whole nightmare go away.

We want to hide from people. The thought of going to the shopping center creates fear because we feel everyone there looking at us knows we are a failure. We feel like the words, "I Am Divorced!" have been stamped on our foreheads, so naturally we want to hide from people, even our close friends.

No one wants to admit it is over. We say, "Oh, she will be back. He'll come home. I just know it!" Because we can't admit that it is over, we try to convince ourselves differently. But we are divorced; there is no tomorrow for our marriage; none of the plans made together for the future will ever come true. That is an extremely difficult realization and therefore it is natural to go through a period of denial when getting a divorce.

However, as long as you remain at the step of denial, you will never make any progress in your recovery. This is difficult to accept (especially if you are presently midst a divorce proceeding), but I want to tell you as lovingly as I know how that it is over. You are divorced! She is not coming back. He won't be returning. Until you accept the finality of the facts you cannot travel on the road to recovery. I know this because I lived it. And I have talked to many people and met with many counselors who agree. You must accept the divorce before healing can begin.

The denial step is a long way from the ideal of recovery. But I want to assure you, reconciliation is possible. It may be difficult to admit it is over, but there is hope for hurting people, and you can have a happy future.

Step Two: Loneliness
Learning to deal with loneliness is a second step taken toward divorce recovery. During a marriage relationship one is rarely alone. And even when your mate is gone for a time, you know it is temporary. However, realizing your mate won't return is one of the most agonizing experiences of getting a divorce. One of the reasons many people stay at step one (denial) so long is an unwillingness to deal with the loneliness that comes in accepting their mate's farewell.

During the marriage your mate was always there. You ate, worked, played, cried, and planned together. But now you are alone.

Where once there was activity, there is now only lonely silence. Meal times are spent in solitude. And so you hurt. At night the bed seems strangely roomy. And so you hurt. During the day you dread the nights, and in the evenings you dread the coming day. You feel so empty. Like no other time in your life, you feel totally alone.

You feel that no one understands what you're going through. No one could hurt the way you are hurting. Thus you feel even more alone.

This response only perpetuates the loneliness. You are hurting because you are alone, but at the same time you still hide from people. Old friends no longer call, and couple-friends no longer come around. But the last thing you want to do is make new friends (because they might find out you're divorced!).

As hard as this step may seem, it holds the key to overcoming loneliness. To stop this isolation you must first get out of the house. Call someone, anyone, and go out for a hamburger, or for a hike. Don't turn inward, reach out to others and start being with people again.

Yes, you will be afraid. It isn't easy. You'd rather just go to bed or watch a TV rerun. But ask yourself a question. Do you like being lonely?

I can tell you from experience that unless you decide to overcome your loneliness you never will. There are many people stranded at this step. Don't get stuck here. You must take the first step. Reach out to others and get involved with life again.

In Joshua 1:5 God promised Joshua, "As I was with Moses, so I will be with you; I will never leave you nor forsake you." Isn't that exciting? God pledges to never abandon us. Others can neglect us, but God *never* will. We may try to leave God, but He promises to never forsake us.

That is a great promise. It has brought comfort and reassurance to me. Meditate on that verse and let God assure you that He is with you. He is there and He is not silent. In times of loneliness He will help you; He will be your friend.

Step Three: Guilt
As the reality of the divorce sinks in and you are faced with accepting its reality, you will experience strong feelings of guilt. The newly divorced often begin believing they are bad

people. You may convince yourself that the divorce was all your fault. Words may echo in your mind, "If only I had done this or that."

These feelings of guilt trigger a chain reaction that cause people to doubt their right to happiness. You start thinking you deserve to be hurting, lonely, and miserable. Since you are convinced of your own worthlessness, you begin thinking that God and the whole world hates you.

Guilt will destroy you if you don't deal with it. You must admit your mistakes. The divorce was partly your fault (maybe mostly your fault). But remember, in almost every instance, both mates are to blame where a divorce occurs.

No progress toward recovery can be made as long as guilt impedes grace. The truth is that God loves us, even though we aren't perfect (Rom. 5:8). We must first accept God's love and then accept ourselves. Making a mistake does not mean God will reject us. Guilt is a signal we need to ask God's forgiveness for past mistakes. If we ask He promises to forgive (1 John 1:9). This is the only answer, for no amount of self-punishment will remove the feelings of guilt. Self-punishment only reinforces guilt feelings and perpetuates the need for more punishment.

If you are at this step get off the emotional torture rack. You must accept your past mistakes and imperfect nature, recognizing that though you are only human, God loves you anyway. Forgiveness is the avenue out of guilt in taking the next step on the road to recovery.

Step Four: Rejection
When going through a divorce, if your mate left you, then there will be especially strong feelings of rejection. It hurts deeply to realize your mate no longer cares.

None of us handle rejection well. We all have a need to be accepted. When rejected you will begin seeing yourself negatively. Tempted to compare yourself with others, you will think them better than you. Instead of seeing yourself as a special person, you view yourself as a zero with no appreciable qualities.

To overcome feelings of rejection you must realize your individuality. You are a unique individual with qualities and gifts that set you apart from others. You have an original personality. There is not another person in the world like you. God made you as a special person. You have a lot to offer people and to life itself. God has a purpose for your life and a good plan (Jer. 29:11-12). As soon as you realize this you will be ready to move on the road toward recovery.

Step Five: Grief

You will have to learn to effectively deal with grief in climbing toward recovery. First of all, it is just as natural to grieve the loss of a mate due to divorce as it is due to death. During this time of grief it is natural to exhibit a wide range of emotional reactions. You may be repulsed by food and lose a considerable amount of weight. At times you may burst out crying unexpectedly. And the tears will seem to flow uncontrollably. But it's okay to cry; it's okay to hurt. It's normal to feel the pains of grief.

However, at some point in time the days of mourning must come to an end. Life must go on. Yes, have your time of grief. Cry, mourn, and experience the pain and hurt. But don't wallow in it. Don't carry it with you for the rest of your life. There are too many steps left on the road to recovery to be waylaid here. It will be impossible to continue until grief is left behind.

You must accept the fact of the marriage's demise. It is over. Stop living in the past and begin looking to the future. Be thankful for the past good years and times, but realize that they are just that—past. It is finished; accept that fact. Cherish the good times, but for your own emotional well-being and positive future, don't dwell on the past. Living in the past will destroy your future. When you are ready to let go of the past and look to the future, only then will you be ready to continue.

Step Six: Fear

Now we are ready to tackle the next step on the way to divorce recovery—fear. Realizing you must let go of the past can be a very fearful experience, especially for someone who has just gone through a divorce.

You were comfortable with the old life. You knew what to expect and what was expected of you. Plans for the future were in motion and they were coming to pass. But now that is suddenly gone. After divorce one often doesn't have plans for the future. You may not know what is expected in your new role as a "single" person. You have lots of unanswered questions. Financial security may be a luxury of the past. You may have to go to work to support yourself, or look for a higher-salaried job to offset the loss of a second income. To put it simply, you are afraid.

Fear is natural because you have never been in this position. So let me assure you, it is not wrong to be fearful. However, it will be detrimental if you allow fear to keep you from progressing to recovery. You must overcome your fear. You may say, "But how can I overcome my fear? I'm afraid, and I don't know what to do!"

First, don't try to solve the problems by yourself. Invite God to help you and He will. All He needs is an invitation. God's promises helped me to realize that He was protecting me in my time of crisis, and I need not fear anything. Notice what He says, "So do not fear, for I am with you, do not be dismayed, for I am your God. I will strengthen you and help you; I will uphold you with My righteous right hand" (Isa. 41:10).

What a promise that is! He will strengthen and help us; therefore, we need not fear. To suddenly be forced into living alone can be a fearful thing. I would encourage those who are to read Psalm 91 as an example of the physical protection God promises. It is comforting to follow a personal God who watches over and protects us from danger and who strengthens and helps us to face the future.

It is time to put your trust in God and realize you don't have to solve your problems alone. Start looking to the future with expectancy. And as soon as you are ready to, then you can continue your climb to recovery.

Step Seven: Anger

Another common emotion that usually follows grief and fear is that of anger. During my camping trip with Vern Masterson, he said, "One minute I want to beg her to take me back, and the next minute I'm so angry I don't ever want to see her again!"

Those who go through a divorce experience a great deal of anger. They become angry at their mate for causing the hurt. They become angry at themselves for letting this happen. And finally, they become angry at God, because somehow they feel He is responsible.

Like Vern Masterson, you may have felt so much anger toward your mate that you wanted to kill. Or you may have been so mad at yourself that you considered taking your own life. And in your anger toward God, you might have done and said things that you later regretted.

You must rid yourself of this anger. If you don't, it will turn to bitterness and eventually destroy you from the inside out (Eph. 4:31). As long as you focus on anger you cannot make progress. Anger will sap your emotional strength. It will cause you to harbor negative feelings and attitudes that only feed your emotional pain and frustration. Anger will hold back and cheat you from obtaining the full life that can be yours.

Forgiveness is the key to dealing with your anger. You must forgive your mate. You must pardon yourself. And you must absolve any other person you feel contributed to the divorce. Experience has taught me that this is not easy. But without forgiveness anger reigns supreme and recovery is a fleeting dream.

Step Eight: Resentment

The next step, resentment, goes hand-in-hand with anger. While anger involves feelings of hostility and frequently stimulates us to take aggressive action toward another, resentment, the result of strong feelings of hurt, usually causes us to retreat from the source of pain and injury.

During a divorce, we often build up deep indignation toward

others and, as a result, attempt to avoid those who are hurting us. We may start resenting our children, family, coworkers, or friends because of what they've said or done. These resentments frequently cause us to avoid those closest to us and can lead to feelings of anger which, in turn, may produce hostility toward those who have hurt us.

Don't harbor those resentments. Deal with them. Find out the cause of your indignation and deal with it. If your resentments have caused you to say or do things to offend others, then go to them and correct the problem.

Dealing with the anger and resentment by asking for forgiveness will begin the healing of hurts and emotional pains. This healing must take place before you move to the next step and recovery.

Step Nine: Forgiveness

Forgiveness is perhaps the most critical step along the road to recovery. In fact, without forgiveness you will never experience total recovery. I have met people who have been divorced for over 10 years and are still harboring hate and bitterness. All of these people were miserable and unfulfilled in their lives. Don't let that happen to you. Don't miss out on a positive and rewarding future just because you were unwilling to forgive.

You may never be able to restore the relationship you desire, but you certainly can forgive those involved and allow your own emotions to begin healing. Forgiveness is the best medicine for hurting emotions. Full and final forgiveness will allow you to take the final steps toward recovery. Don't delay those who need your forgiveness. You've come too far to stop now.

Step Ten: Acceptance

Once you have been able to forgive, you are well on your way to recovery. It is now time to accept your new position and place in life. If you take time to look back you will see how far you have come on this climb to recovery. When you were struggling with denial you thought there was no way you would ever make it. Now here you are, almost to the end of recovery.

It is time to look life squarely in the face. You have learned a lot about yourself, and you will continue to grow. You aren't the same person you were going into the divorce. Caught between rocks and some hard places, you have made the right decisions. Finally you can offer the gift of forgiveness to those who have hurt you deeply.

Now you must accept the past as gone forever and the future as limitless. God is your true friend; He has not left you to fight your battle alone. At this stage you must work on being content with yourself and your circumstances (Phil. 4:11). You must not force things to happen or rush into things. Seek guidance from God concerning the plans and decisions you make as you begin to recover (Psalm 32:8). As you learn to accept your circumstances in life, you'll soon discover you're ready for the next step.

Step Eleven: Self-Security

The end is in sight. You are almost there. You have almost accomplished what you never expected to achieve. There is only one step left. You must learn to be self-secure. Believe in yourself. Learn to accept and like yourself just the way you are.

You are a very special person. God made you in His image (Gen. 1:27). You have grown through your mistakes and the hard times. And you have not only survived, but developed a better understanding of your own weaknesses and strengths.

In working through the recovery process you have learned how deeply God loves you. And since He loves you, this instills a sense of worthiness.

You have learned to respect yourself, even with all your weaknesses. You are the only you there is in all of the world. No other person on earth is like you. God made you the way you are for a reason, be encouraged. He has special things for you to do in this life. And He will help you accomplish them.

You have a right to feel secure with who, what, and where

you are as well as what the future holds. As long as you allow God to control your life you will experience His best for you. Even after all you have gone through you can now be self-secure, because God has a plan for your life.

Yes, there are many unanswered questions. You haven't "arrived." There are still problems and recurrent feelings to be faced, but you have learned that you're not alone. God will be with you as you continue to weave in and out of the stages of recovery. Therefore, you have a right to be secure with your self and with your current place in life.

Step Twelve: Recovery

The road to recovery is a rough and erratic trek. Some never even start. Others begin, but give up along the way.

Recovery takes time. For most it means lots of time. The time it takes isn't nearly as important as what you learn along the way. There is something to learn about yourself, God, and others at each stage you take in the journey. Learn all you can. As you take each step you'll discover that the problems you face are there to provoke your growth as a person. Recovering, you will be prepared to accomplish new things that will make your life meaningful and rewarding (James 1:2-4).

Recovery doesn't mean you have made it in life. It means you are now ready to start living. Recovery is a place of beginnings; it's not the end of the climb. It is the state of mind in which we are ready to honestly tell God, "Thanks, for this day! You have made it for me because You love me and have good things in store for my life today. In the days to come, I am ready and willing to do what You have planned for me." Unfortunately, many people go through their entire lives never able to make such a declaration. But as you continue to invite God to direct the decisions of your life you will discover that what Jesus said is true. "The thief comes only to steal and kill and destroy; I have come that they may have life, and have it to the full" (John 10:10).

So what are you waiting for? Take that first step on the way to recovery where life has the potential for fulfillment again.

LOVE: MEDICINE THAT HEALS THE HURTS

12

As we have seen throughout the book, deteriorating relationships cause severe emotional stress, frustration, and pain. But divorce hurts even worse. And the greater the emotional pain, the more it affects our ability to give and receive love.

During the weekend I spent with Vern we talked a lot about his feelings and the important role love plays in our lives. Vern was concerned about his growing mistrust of people and increasing lack of patience. He said, "Myron, I find myself withdrawing more and more from people. The only reason I agreed to come with you this weekend was because it was a chance to get out of town and away from people." He paused and apologetically said, "I didn't used to be this way. I always liked people. But now, I almost hate being around them."

Vern was not only developing a strong resentment toward people, but was also having a hard time accepting himself. The entire weekend was representative of his mind-set. He continually put himself down, for even the smallest mistake or accident. One morning Vern accidentally spilled his coffee. He immediately began chastising himself, "I am the most clumsy person in the world! I can't do anything right, not even drink a cup of coffee."

It was obvious that his self-image had suffered greatly during the past several months. He was a man living out the pain of a broken relationship.

The Results of Emotional Pain
Emotional pain does more than just hurt. It causes us to react

in many confusing and negative ways that include the following:

- ▶ We mistrust people.
- ▶ We become defensive.
- ▶ We withdraw and isolate ourselves.
- ▶ We lose confidence in ourselves.
- ▶ We tend to blame God.

Obviously there are many other things that could be added to this list, but we have already dealt with many of them in previous chapters. I would like to draw your attention to these five reactions to emotional pain, because they all point to the same problem, the absence of love. The less love there is in our lives, the longer it takes to recover from the pangs of relationship failure.

We mistrust people. Deteriorating relationships cause us to mistrust other people, not just those who hurt us, but all people. We begin questioning motives. If someone tries to be nice to us we start thinking, "What does she want!" Since we have been hurt before, we think we will be again.

As we noted earlier, relationships tend to be governed by the law of cause and effect. Every action tends to produce a reaction. Positive actions cause positive reactions and negative actions in turn, negative reactions. This certainly is the case with emotional pain which naturally leads to a mistrust of others.

However, mistrust is not the real problem, it is only the symptom. We must remember that many of the "actions" we observe are in reality a "reaction" to something else. If you want to solve the real problem you must find out the cause of the reaction and deal with it. You cannot solve relationship problems by fighting reactions. Get to the source of the problem, then move forward. That is the goal of this chapter.

If you have trouble trusting people because of the past then you are experiencing an even bigger problem. Mistrust is a symptom of our lack of love for people. To trust again, you must first learn to love people.

We become defensive. Guarding against being hurt again,

we overreact by ducking when nothing is coming, or striking out for no apparent reason. We build high walls to hide behind in an effort to escape.

As a result, we discover it becomes harder to maintain healthy relationships. Even those people who honestly try to help us through this time find it difficult to continue being a friend.

However, as we will see later, the answer isn't found in dropping our guard. The answer is learning to put love in action. Love reaches out to people. It tears down walls and barriers. With love there is no need to react defensively. Love makes it possible to again share your true self without reservations.

We withdraw and isolate ourselves. I have noticed recently that there are more and more people withdrawing and isolating themselves because of serious relational problems. In talking with people I have learned that the more they isolate themselves, the more bitterness and lack of love there is in their lives. But it isn't the withdrawal that causes the failure to love; just the opposite is true. The absence of love in one's life creates a void. That void is filled with resentment, which in turn causes the withdrawal from people, and sometimes life itself.

The less love there is in our lives, the larger the void. The larger the void, the more bitterness and resentment we hold. As we harbor these negative emotions, the more we withdraw ourselves from others. Just as with mistrust, isolation is only the symptom. The real problem is the absence of love. The more love we have in our lives, the more we want to share it with others. On the other hand, the less love we have, the more we tend to avoid social contact.

We lose confidence in ourselves. People who experience divorce, or other serious relationship problems, usually lose confidence in themselves. Remember Vern who spent several minutes chastising himself over a cup of spilled coffee. People in pain not only lash out at their adversaries, but at themselves as well.

They not only stop loving others, but begin to neglect themselves. This lack of self-confidence reflects the lack of self-love that they are experiencing. People cannot begin rebuilding their self-confidence until they first start accepting themselves again.

We tend to blame God. All of us are tempted to blame God for divorce and relationship problems. But when we blame God, seeing Him as the problem, we begin to withdraw from His presence.

We show anger instead of love toward God. We show resentment instead of appreciation toward Him. All of these are symptomatic of the lack of love in our lives. Blaming God for problems is an accurate indicator of the absence of love in one's life. "God is love. Whoever lives in love lives in God, and God in him" (1 John 4:16). This tells that God is love. We need to stop blaming Him and instead invite Him into our lives. His love is the remedy for the pains that prevent us from healing and leading healthy and happy lives again.

Learning to Love Again

What images come to your mind when you think of learning to love again? Those images reveal your definition and attitude toward love. When you think of learning to love again, can you see yourself as happy and fulfilled, maybe in a new relationship? Is love the thing you need to make you happy and complete? If these are the things you visualize, then you probably have the wrong concept of love.

Most people view love as a means to an end. That is, they want love because it meets a need and does something for them. This is a flawed understanding of love. *The focus of real love is not on yourself, but on others.* Thus, if you want love because it meets your needs, you are actually seeking self-love, and not the true love that comes from God.

God's love is the medicine that heals hurting emotions. Self-love was the cause of damaged emotions. You don't want to fall into the old habits and routines that created the problems in the first place.

People in pain need to experience and practice true love. True love involves the giving and sharing *of* self, not the getting and receiving *for* self that is deified by our society today.

Practicing True Love

The Bible tells us how to practice true love. Earlier we referred to 1 Corinthians 13; however, we now need to take a closer look at Paul's explanation of and exhortation to love. The first three verses of the passage tell us just how important true love is in our lives:

> If I had the gift of being able to speak in other languages without learning them, and could speak in every language there is in all of heaven and earth, but didn't love others, I would only be making noise. If I had the gift of prophecy and knew all about what is going to happen in the future, knew everything about *everything,* but didn't love others, what good would it do? Even if I had the gift of faith so that I could speak to a mountain and make it move, I would still be worth nothing at all without love. If I gave everything I have to poor people, and if I were burned alive for preaching the Gospel but didn't love others, it would be of no value whatever (1 Cor. 13:1-3, TLB).

What a powerful statement concerning the value and importance of love! Meditate on the message of these verses and allow it to sink deep into your heart and soul. It's amazing that we spend such little time developing and applying love in our lives, and yet nothing can compare to its worth and value.

Let's further explore the definitions of love according to this classic chapter. We will then determine the actions needed to bring authentic love into our lives and begin the recovery from past pains that keep us from experiencing present pleasure in our relationships.

Love is very patient and kind, never jealous or envious,

never boastful or proud, never haughty or selfish or rude. Love does not demand its own way. It is not irritable or touchy. It does not hold grudges and will hardly even notice when others do it wrong. It is never glad about injustice, but rejoices whenever truth wins out. If you love someone you will be loyal to him no matter what the cost. You will always believe in him, always expect the best of him, and always stand your ground in defending him. All the special gifts and powers from God will some-day come to an end, but love goes on forever (1 Cor. 13:4-8, TLB).

This is one of the most succinct descriptions of love ever written. It tells us what love is, and what it is not. Notice that the descriptions of love represent a positive action taken to-ward someone else. It is very clear that love involves doing things for others, instead of having others do things for us. Love is made up of the things we do in serving and meeting the needs of others.

The Healing Power of Love in Action

Love is an *action*. The actions of love bring healing to our body, mind, and emotions. Most of us think that our emotion-al hurts are cured by "being loved." Even though we need to be loved by others, it is our sharing of love with others that becomes the healing medicine that allows us to recover and lead productive lives. Let's look more closely at each of the actions of love as presented in 1 Corinthians 13:4-8.

Love is very patient. To begin healing your hurting emo-tions you must learn to practice patience with others and yourself. Patience is defined by *Webster's New World Dictio-nary* as, "showing calm endurance." Patience is the result of being at peace with yourself, the situation, and the other person. It accepts the mistakes of others without retaliation. It is a demonstration of your willingness to put the other per-son's concerns ahead of your own.

Patience allows you to relax emotionally, even during trying and difficult circumstances. It prevents the body from becoming uptight and tense and helps prevent stress. Work at practicing patience. Work at calming your spirit and emotions when things aren't going the way you want. Plan by focusing on serving the best interests of the other person, instead of on how the situation is failing to serve you.

Love produces kind actions. Kindness soothes the emotions like a mother's hand comforts a baby. Kindness reflects gentle and peaceful internal emotions. It is difficult to be kind to another when you are not at peace. Kindness seeks to treat the other person in the way you would want to be treated in that same situation (Matt. 7:12).

Performing acts of kindness for others helps alleviate the tensions and pressures that exist between people. It helps restore hurting relationships and damaged emotions. Therefore, be committed to treating others with kindness. As you meet their needs and treat them the way you want to be treated, you will begin to view yourself differently.

Kindness always helps promote peace between people. Peace between individuals helps heal the emotional hurts and pains.

Love is never jealous or envious. If you want to remove your emotional hurts strive to avoid jealousy and envy. Jealous people are suspicious people. And suspicious people are continually worrying and fretting inside. They are people who are afraid to trust others.

Jealousy creates urges for revenge. It focuses on undermining relationships instead of restoring them. It keeps your emotions in turmoil. Jealousy focuses on and promotes self instead of serving others. It feeds hurting emotions and causes ill-feelings to fester, instead of helping heal the hurts. It is antagonistic instead of peaceful. Jealousy promotes conflict instead of finding solutions. If you wish to heal your hurting emotions, avoid jealousy at all cost.

Love is never boastful or proud. Boastful and proud people are more concerned about their own wants and desires than those of others. Boastful, proud people are extremely self-centered individuals. And remember, it was self-centeredness that led us away from a cooperation relationship style into increasing conflicts.

Love focuses attention on others instead of self. Its goal is to please others, and build them up, not build up and promote self.

Love is never haughty or selfish or rude. Rudeness is the epitome of self-centeredness. Rudeness demonstrates a total lack of concern for others. Haughty people by their actions communicate that they are better and more deserving than those around them. Such actions will only drive people away and leave one more lonely and hurting than ever.

Love does not demand its own way. People who always demand doing things their own way eventually wind up getting to do those things by themselves. Demanding "your way" is one of the surest ways to end up alone.

Focus instead on how you can get involved with others and support them in accomplishing their way. Rather than leading to loneliness, promoting others' ideas and ways will befriend you to many people. As you are a friend to others, and help them carry out their plans, you will discover that they, in turn, will be more eager to return the favor and help you accomplish your plans.

Love is not irritable or touchy. People who practice love are compatible. They don't carry chips on their shoulders. Love exercises self-control and does not strike back with cutting remarks when offended.

Are you easily irritated? This is a common trait of the self-centered person. When things don't go your way, you are prone to pout. Your actions help drive people away from you. No one likes to be around irritable or touchy people. They are very unpredictable and difficult to please.

People who are easily irritated are not in control of their emotions; they are letting their emotions control their actions.

Love does not hold grudges and will hardly even notice when others do it wrong. When you practice love, you don't keep track of offenses. Instead of criticizing others when they make a mistake, you are there to help them with their problem. Never seek revenge or attempt to get even when you are wronged. Love is marked by a forgiving spirit, and is quick to forget the mistakes of others.

Never throw the mistakes of others in their faces as a means of supporting your own "righteousness." You hurt when others hurt and are always eager to help where needed.

Love is never glad about injustice, but always promotes truth and honesty. If you are going to practice love you will never be glad when others are taken advantage of, or unjustly treated. You will promote truth, honesty, and fairness in every situation.

You will never take advantage of another person, even when you could without them knowing about it. Trusted to treat everyone equally, you will never deliberately show favoritism.

Love is always loyal, no matter what the cost. When applying love to your actions, never use people for your own selfish gain. Instead, loyally and faithfully serve others' needs and you will be counted upon to do what you say you will.

You will not compromise your commitment when it is to your advantage to do so, and you will defend and help others in need, regardless of the attitudes and feelings of public opinion.

Love always believes in, expects the best from, and faithfully defends the honor of others. When you demonstrate love, you positively support the other person and his or her best interest. You have faith in the other person and communicate that faith. Challenge that person to be all she can be. Encourage him to develop his full potential.

When the other person gets discouraged, you are there to encourage, not scoff at their weaknesses. You are always ready to offer personal and public praise for jobs well done.

Love goes on forever. Love must not be conditional. People must not feel the need to perform to earn your love. Communicate that your love is there for the taking without strings attached.

Your actions of love are not based on your approval of the other person's deeds. You must always be there to serve the needs of others. Your service isn't dependent upon them. You love faithfully because it is commanded.

We have just looked at a brief description of love in action as described in 1 Corinthians 13:4-8. Carefully study the actions of love presented in this passage. Make them a part of your life and the way you relate to others. As you do, you will discover that the more you act out what love is, the more love you will get back from others. And the more love others give to you, the more your own needs will be met. This is the wonderful cause and effect cycle of love. In giving, we receive, just as God intended.

We Must Learn to Receive and Give Love

Most of this book has focused, either directly or indirectly, on the importance of serving others' needs as the foundation on which healthy and rewarding relationships are built. This truth can't be overemphasized.

However, it is equally important that we learn to receive love as well as give it. A cooperation relationship style is built on the mutual serving of needs. Thus, it is extremely important that you allow the other person to serve your needs as well.

People who have been through a divorce, or have suffered emotionally from degenerating relationships often tend to become very self-secure (one of the steps in divorce recovery). It is good to be self-secure; however, it becomes detrimental to the development of relationships when we are so independent that we communicate to others, "I need nothing from you."

Three of the most common reasons people tend to have difficulty receiving love from others are as follows:

▶ The need to be in control.
▶ The need not to be indebted to anyone.
▶ The need not to be hurt again.

The need to be in control. Once people have been hurt in a relationship, especially divorce, and able to recover, they tend to feel a strong need to maintain control over their lives. This is especially true of people who feel the other person was responsible for their emotional hurts and pains.

This is a normal and healthy attitude for people who wind up alone following a divorce. However, it becomes unhealthy when maintaining such a need for control interferes with allowing others to serve your needs.

If you are going to develop relationships with others then you must be willing to give up a certain amount of control. You have to provide the other person the right and opportunity to serve you.

Failure to turn loose of the control over your life is one way to insure that future relationships will be just as painful as past.

The need not to be indebted to anyone. Fear of indebtedness is another reason people who have had painful relationships are reluctant to accept love from others. This is a very self-centered, but common reason for rejecting love from another person. Again let me emphasize, when you're alone it is a great strength to be independent, but if you expect to form positive relationships with others, you must be willing to give up some of that independence and become dependent on another.

People need to feel needed. If you are so independent that you don't need anything from anyone, you will suffer failure in future relationships. You must be willing to become vulnerable and show your need for others. Be willing to communicate that need. I can assure you it isn't a sign of weakness, but a sign of maturity.

We all have needs. It is only through the honest sharing and meeting of those needs that we are able to build strong relationships that serve instead of hurt others.

The need not to be hurt again. Some people fear being hurt again and cannot accept love from others. Of course no one wants to be hurt again; however, you must take the risk if you ever expect to experience the benefits of a rich and rewarding relationship again.

Solid relationships are built on trust, not suspicion and fear. You must be willing to trust your feelings with another person and let them trust their's with you. Allowing the fear of being hurt in another relationship to hold you back will insure that you live a lonely existence for the rest of your life. And no one wants to look forward to that possibility.

So I challenge you to open up your life. Share yourself with others and allow them to share themselves with you. God has made you a very special and unique person. He wants you to live life to its fullest. But to do so means that you must be willing to give of yourself.

Remember, there is no such thing as a "perfect" relationship. We all make mistakes. However, it isn't the mistake that is important, it's how we deal with that mistake that counts. We have two choices: we can run and hide when we fail and let life pass us by, or we can learn from our past failures and use them to prepare and equip us for living life in the future to its fullest potential.

I don't know what you will choose, but I chose the latter, and in doing so have learned from life with the Lord that there is not only *hope for hurting relationships,* but hope for hurting people as well!